It's easy 'nough to titter w'en de stew is Smokin' hot
But hit's mighty ha'd to giggle w'en dey's nuffin' in de pot.

Paul Lawrence Dunbar
1872-1906

STEWS

& Soups

by
Joanne Waring Lindeman

Illustrated by Craig Torlucci

© Copyright 1976
Nitty Gritty Productions
Concord, California

A Nitty Gritty Book*
Published by
Nitty Gritty Productions
P.O. Box 5457
Concord, California 94524

*Nitty Gritty Books — Trademark
Owned by Nitty Gritty Productions
Concord, California

ISBN 0-911954-37-6

Library of Congress Cataloging in Publication Data

Lindeman, Joanne Waring.
  Soups & stews.

  Consists of 2 pts., Soups & stews and Stews &
soups, inverted with respect to each other.
  Includes indexes.
    1. Soups. 2. Stews. I. Title. II. Title:
Stews & soups.
TX757.L56   641.8'13   76-27363
ISBN 0-911954-37-6

TABLE OF CONTENTS

INTRODUCTION

Some of the world's best known dishes—Boeuf Bourguignon, Bouillabaisse, Blanquette De Veau and Hungarian Goulash—are stews! A stew, or ragout as it is called in French, can be elegant or a simple family dish.

Economical cuts of meat respond to the slow, moist heat of stewing by becoming succulent and delicious. For beef stew, chuck is the best choice. It has better flavor, usually costs less and requires less cooking time than the usual "stew beef." I prefer buying a chuck roast and cutting it into the size pieces called for in the recipe I'm following. And, there is additional economy when you do the cutting.

When browning meat for stew, don't have the heat too high, and turn the pieces frequently. Gentle browning and slow cooking produce tender morsels of marvelously flavored meat.

Leisurely stews are perfect for entertaining four to forty. They don't require constant supervision and can easily be made in quantity.

Every country has its traditional stews and many of the recipes in this book were collected while traveling in various countries. Some of them are quite unusual. I hope you will like my recipes and enjoy nutritious stew often.

Jeanne Lindeman

SEAFOOD STEWS

BOUILLABAISSE

This traditional French fish stew is perfect for winter time parties.

2 lbs. frozen flounder fillets, thawed
2 onions, sliced
1/3 cup olive oil
1 cup crabmeat
1 can (7-1/2 ozs.) minced clams
12 fresh clams in shells
1 lb. shelled raw shrimp
2 cans (16 ozs. ea.) tomatoes
1 bay leaf
1/2 cup chopped pimiento
1/4 cup parsley
1 tsp. garlic powder
1/2 tsp. each thyme and saffron
1 cup dry white wine
French bread, thickly sliced

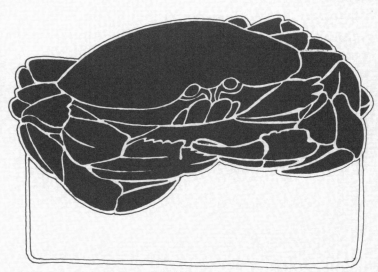

Cut flounder into "fingers." Saute onions in oil until golden. Add flounder, crabmeat, minced clams, clams in shells, shrimp, tomatoes and bay leaf. Bring to boil and cook 15 minutes. Stir in pimiento, parsley, garlic powder, thyme and saffron. Turn heat very low. Add wine. Cover and allow flavors to absorb for 5 minutes. Toast bread under broiler. Place one slice of toasted bread in each bowl. Ladle soup over bread. Makes 8 servings.

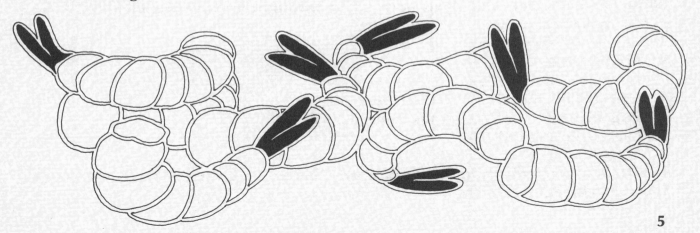

BASQUE CLAMS AND RICE

48 hardshell clams
3 cups water
2 cups raw rice

1 tsp. salt
1/4 cup olive oil
1/4 cup chopped parsley

3 cloves garlic, minced
Butter Sauce, see below

Scrub clams well. Bring water to boil in large kettle. Add rice, salt, olive oil, parsley, garlic and clams. Bring to a boil and reduce heat to very low. Cover and cook 20 to 25 minutes, or until clams open. Serve with Butter Sauce and plenty of French bread. Makes 4 servings.

BUTTER SAUCE

1/2 cup (1/4 lb.) butter
1/4 cup olive oil
3 cloves garlic, minced

3 tbs. lemon juice
1 tbs. minced parsley

Heat all ingredients in small saucepan. Pour into a bowl and serve with Basque Clams and Rice.

6

SCALLOP CREOLE

Delicious served over rice!

1 lb. fresh or frozen scallops
2 tbs. oil
1/2 cup chopped onion
1/2 cup chopped green pepper
1 clove garlic, crushed
1 can (16 ozs.) tomatoes
1 can (8 ozs.) tomato sauce
1 tsp. sugar

salt and lemon pepper
1/4 tsp. thyme
1/4 tsp. basil
1 tsp. Spice Islands Beau Monde Seasoning
1 bay leaf
2 tbs. cornstarch
parsley

Cut scallops into 1-inch pieces. Heat oil in saucepan. Add onion, pepper and garlic. Saute until tender. Stir in tomatoes, tomato sauce, sugar and seasonings. Cover and simmer 15 minutes. Add scallops and simmer 5 minutes. Remove bay leaf. Blend cornstarch with 1/4 cup water. Add to mixture. Cook, stirring until thickened. Garnish with parsley. Makes 4 servings.

CIOPPINO

This fishermen's stew is a favorite in San Francisco. Serve with green salad, sourdough French bread and bibs for everyone. It's somewhat messy to eat, but that's part of the fun!

1/4 cup olive oil
1 large onion, finely chopped
1 can (1 lb. 14 ozs.) tomatoes
1 can (6 ozs.) tomato paste
2 cloves garlic, minced
1-1/4 cups dry white wine
3 cups water

1/2 tsp. <u>each</u> thyme, oregano, basil,
   coarsely ground pepper
1 bay leaf, crumbled
3 Dungeness crabs, cracked
1 lb. scallops
1 lb. small shrimp
24 clams in their shells

Heat olive oil in large pot. Saute onions until lightly browned. Add tomatoes, tomato paste, garlic, wine, water and seasonings. Cover and simmer 2 hours. Cut scallops in half. Shell and devein shrimp. Scrub clams well. Add seafood to sauce and cook 10 minutes or until clams open. Serve seafood in large bowls with sauce poured over. Makes 12 servings.

TURTLE RAGOUT

2 tbs. butter
1 onion, chopped
1 clove garlic, mashed
1 tbs. flour
1 cup water
1 bay leaf
2 lbs. turtle meat, diced
1/4 cup dry sherry

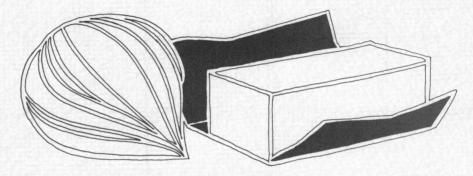

Heat butter in saucepan. Lightly brown onion and garlic. Blend in flour. Gradually add water and stir until smooth. Add bay leaf, turtle meat and sherry. Simmer 1/2 hour. Serve piping hot. Makes 6 servings.

POULTRY AND RABBIT STEWS

CHICKEN AND DUMPLINGS

4 to 5 lb. stewing chicken
1-1/2 qts. boiling water
1 onion, sliced
2 potatoes, quartered
1 carrot, sliced
1 stalk celery, sliced
1 whole clove
4 peppercorns
2 tsp. salt
Fluffy Dumplings, page 13
2 tbs. chopped parsley

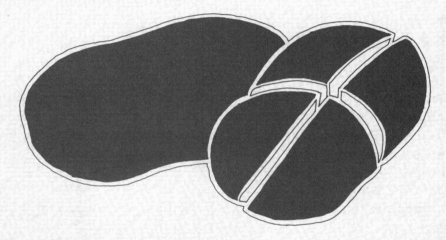

Cut chicken into pieces. Put into large kettle with boiling water, onions and potatoes. Bring to a boil and skim off foam. Reduce heat. Cover and simmer gently 1-1/2 hours or until tender. Lift chicken from pan. When cool enough to handle, remove meat. Discard bones and skin. Return meat to kettle. Add carrots, celery, cloves, peppercorns and salt. Simmer 1/2 hour. Just before serving time, mix dump-

lings. Bring chicken to boil. Drop dumpling mixture by teaspoonfuls onto boiling broth. Cook over low heat 10 minutes. Cover, and cook 10 minutes longer. Do not peek while dumplings are cooking. Serve garnished with parsley. Makes 6 servings.

FLUFFY DUMPLINGS

2 cups biscuit mix
2/3 cup milk
1/4 cup chopped parsley

Combine ingredients in small mixing bowl. Stir until moistened. Drop by rounded teaspoonfuls onto boiling broth. Cook over low heat 10 minutes. Cover, and cook 10 minutes longer. Do not raise lid while dumplings are cooking.

FABULOUS FRICASSEE

2 (2-1/2 to 3 lbs.) frying chickens
4 cups water
1/8 tsp. mace
1 tsp. salt
1/4 tsp. pepper
1 stalk celery, chopped
1 onion, quartered

1 pkg. (10 ozs.) frozen peas
1/4 cup butter
1/4 cup flour
1 cup (1/2 pt.) whipping cream
2 tsp. Angostura bitters
juice of 1 lemon

    Cut chickens into serving pieces. Place in large kettle and cover with water. Stir in mace, salt, pepper, celery and onion. Bring to a boil and simmer 40 minutes. Remove chicken and discard skin. Strain and reserve broth. Discard onion and celery. Add peas to broth. Melt butter in kettle and stir in flour. Gradually add broth and cream. Cook, stirring, until mixture thickens. Add bitters and mix well. Return chicken to saucepan. Bring to a boil. Reduce heat and add lemon juice. Serve at once with mashed potatoes. Makes 6 servings.

ELEGANT CHICKEN STEW

For a special dinner party serve with a chilled bottle of Grey Riesling wine.

1 (3 lbs.) chicken
1/4 cup flour
salt and pepper
1/2 tsp. paprika
2 tbs. oil
2 tbs. butter
5 potatoes, quartered

4 carrots, sliced
1/2 tsp. rosemary
1 can (10-1/2 ozs.) cream of chicken soup
1 can (10-1/2 ozs.) consomme
3 tbs. chopped parsley
1 lb. fresh asparagus

Cut chicken into serving pieces. Remove skin, if desired. Wash pieces and dry on paper toweling. Mix flour with salt, pepper and paprika. Dust chicken with seasoned flour. Heat oil and butter in Dutch oven. Brown chicken on all sides. Add vegetables and rosemary. Combine soups and parsley. Pour over chicken. Cover and simmer 1 hour. Cut asparagus spears in half crosswise. Place pieces in a row down the middle of the stew. Cover and simmer 10 minutes longer. Makes 4 to 6 servings.

BRANDIED CHICKEN STEW

Keep this recipe in mind for your next buffet supper.

5 lbs. chicken pieces
paprika
1/4 cup (1/2 cube) butter
1 envelope dry onion soup mix
2 cans (10 ozs. ea.) chicken stock
1 tsp. marjoram

salt and pepper
1 pkg. (10 ozs.) frozen peas
1 lb. mushrooms, thickly sliced
1/4 cup flour
1 cup heavy cream
1/4 cup brandy

Skin chicken if desired. Dust pieces with paprika. Heat butter in Dutch oven. Brown chicken well on all sides. Combine soup mix, stock, marjoram, salt and pepper. Pour over chicken. Cover and simmer 45 minutes, or until chicken is tender. Remove chicken to platter. Keep warm. Add peas and mushrooms to sauce. Cook 5 minutes. Blend flour with cream and brandy. Add to sauce, stirring until blended. Return chicken to mixture and heat gently 5 minutes. Serve with French rolls and sweet butter. Makes 6 to 8 servings.

BURGUNDY CHICKEN

1 tbs. oil
3 lb. chicken, cut up
1/2 cup brandy
1 onion, sliced
2 cloves garlic, minced
1/2 lb. mushrooms, cut in half
1 tbs. flour
1 cup Burgundy
salt and pepper

Heat oil in large skillet. Brown chicken pieces. Pour in brandy and ignite. When flame subsides, add onion, garlic and mushrooms. Sprinkle with flour and gradually pour wine over all. Add salt and pepper. Simmer 1/2 hour or until chicken is tender. Makes 4 servings.

17

BASQUE CHICKEN

2 tbs. oil
3 lb. chicken, cut up
salt and pepper
2 cloves garlic, minced
1 cup dry white wine
1 can (14 ozs.) chicken broth
1/2 cup water
fresh basil, finely chopped
4 flat anchovy filets, mashed
2 tbs. tomato paste
12 green olives

Heat oil in electric frying pan or large skillet. Brown chicken. Sprinkle with salt and pepper. Add garlic and wine. Cover tightly and simmer very slowly until wine has evaporated. Add chicken broth and water. Cover and simmer until tender, about 30 minutes. Add more water if necessary. Add basil, anchovies, tomato paste and olives. Simmer until sauce is blended. Makes 4 servings.

CHICKEN CREOLE

3 lb. chicken, cut up
1 clove garlic, cut in half
6 slices bacon
1/2 lb. ham, diced
1 onion, chopped
1 can (16 ozs.) tomatoes, drained
1 tbs. chopped parsley
dash Tabasco

1 tsp. thyme
1/2 tsp. savory
1 tsp. salt
1/2 tsp. pepper
2 cups boiling water
2 cups cooked okra
2 tbs. flour

Rub chicken skin with cut cloves of garlic. Cook bacon in large skillet or electric frying pan until crisp. Drain and crumble. Remove all but 1 tablespoon of fat from skillet. Add chicken and brown on all sides. Remove from skillet. Add ham and onions and saute until golden. Return bacon and chicken to skillet along with tomatoes, parsley, Tabasco, thyme, savory, salt, pepper and water. Cover and simmer 45 minutes or until chicken is tender. Add okra and cook 10 minutes. Mix flour with a little water and stir into mixture. Cook until thickened. Serve with rice. Makes 4 servings.

CHICKEN CACCIATORE WITH VERMICELLI

3 lb. chicken, cut up
2 tbs. butter
1 onion, chopped
2 cloves garlic, mashed
1 can (15 ozs.) spaghetti sauce with meat
1-1/4 cups water
1 cup sliced carrots
1 cup broken vermicelli
salt and pepper
3 tbs. chopped parsley

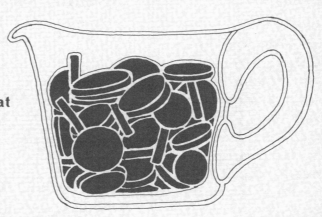

Skin chicken. Melt butter in large skillet. Saute chicken on all sides until golden. Add onion and garlic. Saute 5 minutes. Gradually blend in spaghetti sauce and water. Cover and simmer 15 minutes. Add carrots, vermicelli, salt and pepper to taste. Cover and simmer 20 minutes. Garnish with chopped parsley. Makes 4 servings.

MEXICAN STEW

2 tbs. oil
3 lb. chicken, cut up
1-1/2 tbs. chili powder
1/4 tsp. cinnamon
2 tbs. grated onion
1 tsp. salt
1 can (20 ozs.) pineapple chunks, undrained
2 bananas, quartered
1 avocado, sliced
1/2 lb. white seedless grapes
cooked rice

Heat oil in large skillet or electric frying pan. Slowly brown chicken on all sides. Sprinkle chicken with chili powder, cinnamon, onion and salt. Add pineapple and juice. Cover and simmer 45 minutes. Add water if necessary. Arrange bananas, avocados and grapes over chicken. Serve with rice. Makes 4 servings.

GREEK CHICKEN STEW

1/4 cup butter
3 lb. chicken, cut up
2 onions, finely chopped
1 clove garlic, minced
1 can (16 ozs.) tomatoes
1 tbs. tomato paste
salt and pepper
2 cinnamon sticks
2 cups water
6 potatoes, quartered
1 lb. fresh peas, shelled
1 lb. green beans, 2-inch pieces

Heat butter in large kettle. Brown chicken, onions and garlic. Stir in tomatoes, tomato paste, salt, pepper, cinnamon sticks and water. Bring to boil. Add remaining ingredients. Reduce heat and simmer, covered, 1 hour or until chicken is tender. Remove cinnamon sticks. Makes 6 servings.

23

HAWAIIAN CHICKEN STEW

1 can (9 ozs.) pineapple chunks
1 can (11 ozs.) mandarin oranges
1/2 cup flour
1 tsp. ginger
1 tsp. curry powder
1 tsp. garlic powder
salt and pepper
3 lb. chicken, cut up
1/2 cup (1 cube) butter
1 tbs. lemon juice
2 tart apples
1/3 cup brandy
watercress

Drain juices from canned fruit. Set aside. Combine flour, ginger, curry, garlic powder, salt and pepper in a paper bag. Add chicken pieces and shake to evenly coat. Save remaining flour. Melt butter in large skillet. Brown chicken well on all sides.

Remove browned chicken to baking dish. Gradually add flour mixture to pan drippings, stirring until smooth. Slowly add fruit juices, stirring constantly until smooth. Simmer until thickened. Peel and slice apples. Scatter apple slices, pineapple and oranges over chicken. Sprinkle with lemon juice. Pour sauce over all. Cover and bake in 350°F oven 1 hour. At serving time heat brandy. Pour over chicken and ignite. When flames die out, serve garnished with parsley. Makes 4 servings.

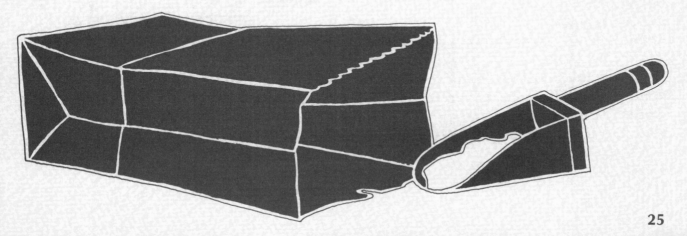

ITALIAN-STYLE CHICKEN

1 tbs. olive oil
3 lb. chicken, cut up
2 cloves garlic, crushed
1 onion, sliced
1/2 lb. fresh mushrooms
1 tbs. flour
1 cup dry white wine
salt and pepper
1 pkg. (10 ozs.) Birds Eye frozen Italian-style vegetables

Heat oil in skillet and brown chicken. Add garlic, onion and mushrooms. Stir in flour. Blend in wine, salt and pepper. Cover and simmer 1/2 hour or until chicken is tender. Add vegetables and cook, uncovered, until sauce cubes are blended. Reduce heat. Cover and simmer 2 minutes. Serve immediately. Makes 4 servings.

RABBIT CHASSEUR

1 rabbit, cut up
3 tbs. flour
salt and pepper
1/4 cup olive oil
2 onions, finely chopped
2 tbs. parsley
2 tbs. minced shallots or
   1 clove garlic, minced

1 tsp. Bovril meat extract
1 tsp. tomato paste
1 tbs. flour
1 tsp. Spice Islands Bouquet Garni
1 cup chicken stock
1/2 cup dry red wine
1/2 lb. mushrooms, sliced
2 tbs. brandy

Wash rabbit and pat dry with paper toweling. Combine flour, salt and pepper. Dredge rabbit in flour. Heat oil in large pot. Brown rabbit on all sides. Remove from pan. Saute onions, parsley and shallots in drippings about 5 minutes. Remove pan from heat and stir in Bovril, tomato paste, flour, Bouquet Garni and more salt if needed. Stir until smooth. Blend in stock and wine. Return rabbit to pan. Cover. Simmer over low heat 40 minutes. Add mushrooms and brandy. Simmer, uncovered, 10 minutes longer. Serve garnished with parsley. Makes 4 servings.

BEEF STEWS

DRESDEN BEEF STEW

If your family is small, freeze half of this flavorful stew for a future meal.

4 lbs. (1-inch thick) round steak
4 tbs. butter
1 tbs. oil
2 large onions, sliced
2 tsp. curry powder
1 tsp. grated fresh ginger
2 tbs. Worcestershire sauce

1 clove garlic, crushed
salt and pepper
1 cup dry white wine
2 cups (1 pt.) sour cream
2 tbs. prepared horseradish
1/4 cup chopped parsley

Cut meat into 1-inch cubes. Heat butter and oil in Dutch oven. Brown meat. Add onions and brown. Stir in curry, ginger, Worcestershire, garlic, salt, pepper and wine. Cover and bake in 300°F oven 3 hours or until meat is tender. Combine sour cream and horseradish. Stir into stew just before serving. Heat but do not allow to boil. Garnish with parsley. Makes 8 to 10 servings.

EASY WINE STEW

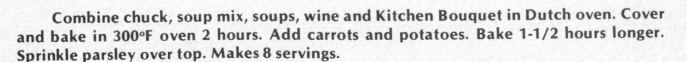

This stew goes together quickly because the meat is not browned first. Serve with hot biscuits and your favorite tossed salad.

4 lb. chuck roast, cubed
1 pkg. (1-3/8 ozs.) dry onion soup mix
1 can (10-1/2 ozs.) golden mushroom soup
1 can (10-1/2 ozs.) cream of mushroom soup
1-2/3 cups Burgundy wine
2 tbs. Kitchen Bouquet
5 carrots, peeled and sliced
5 potatoes, peeled and quartered
chopped parsley

Combine chuck, soup mix, soups, wine and Kitchen Bouquet in Dutch oven. Cover and bake in 300°F oven 2 hours. Add carrots and potatoes. Bake 1-1/2 hours longer. Sprinkle parsley over top. Makes 8 servings.

WINE-GLAZED BEEF STEW

2-1/2 lb. chuck roast
2 tbs. butter
1 clove garlic, minced
1 onion, chopped
salt and pepper
1 can (10-1/2 ozs.) tomato soup
3/4 cup Burgundy wine

1/4 cup water
1/4 tsp. basil
1/4 tsp. thyme
1/2 cup catsup
3 carrots, sliced 1/2-inch
1-1/2 cups celery, cut 1-inch
4 peeled potatoes quartered

Cut meat into 1-1/2 inch cubes. Melt butter in Dutch oven. Brown meat well on all sides. Add garlic and onion. Saute until onion is transparent. Add salt and pepper. Stir in soup, wine and water. Cover and bake in 350°F oven 30 minutes. Add basil, thyme and catsup. Arrange carrots, celery and potatoes on top of meat. Reduce oven temperature to 300°F and bake stew 1-1/2 to 2 hours, or until meat is tender. Makes 4 servings.

BABY BEEF STEW

This delicious creamy stew uses the new "baby beef" or "calf" that is now being sold in most supermarkets, and the combination of flavors is perfect.

2 lb. baby beef roast
2 tbs. butter
1 onion, sliced
1 cup sliced celery
2 cups beef stock

1/8 tsp. thyme
salt and pepper
2 cups cooked cauliflowerets
1 can (4 ozs.) sliced mushrooms
1 cup (1/2 pt.) sour cream

Cut beef into 1-inch cubes. Remove excess moisture with paper toweling. Melt butter in Dutch oven. Brown beef on all sides. Add onion slices, celery, stock, thyme, salt and pepper. Cover and simmer 1 hour or until meat is tender. Add well-drained cauliflowerets, mushrooms and sour cream. Heat, but do not boil, 10 minutes. Makes 4 servings.

BOEUF BOURGUIGNON

Traditionally served with boiled potatoes.

4-1/2 lb. lean boneless chuck roast
1/4 cup salad oil
1/2 lb. salt pork, diced
2 carrots, sliced
3 cloves garlic, minced
1/4 cup flour
2 cups beef stock
2 cups dry red wine

2 tbs. tomato paste
1 bay leaf
1 tsp. thyme
salt and pepper
24 small boiling onions, peeled
1/4 cup butter
1 lb. small button mushrooms
parsley

Trim meat and cut into 1-1/2 inch cubes. Pat cubes with paper toweling to remove excess moisture. Heat oil in Dutch oven. Add salt pork and beef cubes a few at a time. Brown well on all sides. Remove meat as it browns. Add sliced carrots and garlic. Saute 5 minutes. Return meat to pan. Add flour a tablespoon at a time. Stir after each addition. Add beef stock, wine, tomato paste, bay leaf, thyme, salt and pepper. Bring to a

boil. Cover and bake in 350°F oven 2 hours. While meat is cooking, saute onions in butter 10 minutes. Skim fat from meat and add onions. Cook 1/2 hour longer. Saute mushrooms in butter remaining from onions. Add to meat. Serve garnished with parsley. Makes 8 servings.

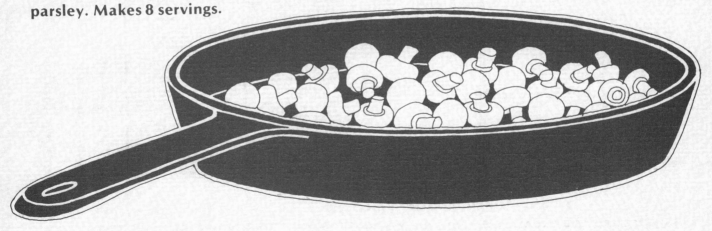

BEEF 'N DUMPLING STEW

Make this pretty stew in your nicest bake-and-serve casserole.

2 to 2-1/2 lb. chuck roast
1 can (10-1/2 ozs.) cream of chicken soup
1 can (10-1/2 ozs.) onion soup
1 can (4 ozs.) sliced mushrooms, drained
1 bay leaf
salt and pepper
1 tbs. Worcestershire sauce
1/3 cup flour
1 pkg. (10 ozs.) frozen peas
4 green pepper rings
Parsley Dumplings, page 37

Cut meat into 1-inch cubes. Place in 3 quart casserole. Combine soups, mushrooms, bay leaf, salt, pepper, Worcestershire and flour. Pour over meat. Cover and bake in 350°F oven 2 hours. Remove from oven. Increase temperature to 400°F.

Remove bay leaf and sprinkle peas over stew. Place pepper rings in center of pan. Drop dumpling mixture by teaspoonfuls around pepper rings. Cover and bake 20 minutes. Makes 4 servings.

PARSLEY DUMPLINGS

1 egg
1/3 cup milk
1 tbs. parsley flakes
2 tbs. oil
1 cup flour
1-1/2 tsp. baking powder
1/2 tsp. salt

Combine ingredients in small mixing bowl. Stir until moistened. Drop by rounded teaspoonfuls onto hot stew. Cover and bake in 400°F oven 20 minutes.

STIFADO

A well-seasoned Greek stew combining chunks of beef, little onions and walnut halves.

3-1/2 lb. chuck roast
1/4 cup butter
1 tsp. pickling spices
1 can (8 ozs.) tomato sauce
1 clove garlic, minced
1 bay leaf

2 tbs. wine vinegar
salt and pepper
water
2 lbs. small white onions
1 cup walnut halves

Trim meat and cut into 1-inch cubes. Heat butter in Dutch oven. Brown meat on all sides. Tie pickling spices in a small piece of cheese cloth. Add to meat along with tomato sauce, garlic, bay leaf, vinegar, salt, pepper and enough water to cover meat. Bring to a boil. Cover and simmer 1-1/2 hours, or until meat is tender. Add onions. Cover and cook until onions are tender, about 20 minutes. Remove pickling spices. Add walnut halves and simmer 10 minutes. Makes 6 servings.

RADOS' STEW

Thank you, Angie, for sharing your favorite Serbian stew.

2-1/2 lb. chuck roast
4 slices bacon, diced
4 onions, quartered
1 clove garlic, minced
2 tsp. salt
1 tsp. pepper

1/2 tsp. marjoram
1 cup dry white wine
1/2 cup water
2 cups (1 pt.) sour cream
chopped parsley
paprika

Trim meat and cut into 1-inch cubes. Saute bacon in large saucepan until crisp. Remove and drain on paper toweling. Brown meat on all sides in bacon drippings. Stir in onion and garlic. Saute 5 minutes. Add salt, pepper, marjoram, wine and water. Bring to boil and simmer 1-1/2 hours or until meat is tender. Add more wine if mixture becomes too dry. Stir in bacon and sour cream. Sprinkle with parsley and paprika. Makes 4 servings.

AFRICAN GROUNDNUT STEW

2 lb. beef chuck roast
2 tbs. peanut oil
2 onions, chopped
2 garlic cloves, crushed
3 large tomatoes, peeled
1 tbs. canned green chiles

salt and pepper
4 cups boiling water
4 beef bouillon cubes
1 cup chunk-style peanut butter
1/2 cup chopped peanuts
parsley

Trim fat from meat and cut into-1 inch cubes. Heat oil in Dutch oven. Brown meat on all sides. Add onions and garlic. Cook 2 minutes. Chop tomatoes and chiles. Add to meat mixture along with salt and pepper. Dissolve bouillon cubes in water. Add to meat. Stir in peanut butter until blended. Cover and simmer gently 1-1/2 hours or until meat is tender. Uncover and simmer 10 minutes longer. If desired, stew may be thickened with a mixture of 1/2 cup cold water and 3 tablespoons flour. Stir thickening into stew. Cook, stirring, until stew comes to a boil and thickens. Garnish with peanuts and parsley and serve. Makes 4 to 6 servings.

BRAZILIAN BEEF

Here's a marvelous blend of flavors to tantalize your taste buds.

2-1/2 lb. chuck roast
2 tbs. oil
1 clove garlic, minced
1 onion, chopped
1/4 cup lemon juice
1/2 cup water
1-1/2 tsp. salt
dash pepper
1 small bay leaf
1/2 cup orange marmalade
1 tsp. curry powder
2 oranges, peeled and sectioned
2 bananas, thickly sliced
Almond Rice, page 43

Trim meat and cut into 1-1/2 inch cubes. Heat oil in kettle. Brown meat well on all sides. Add garlic and onion. Saute 3 minutes. Stir in lemon juice, water, salt, pepper and bay leaf. Cover and simmer 1-1/2 hours or until meat is tender. Blend in orange marmalade and curry powder. Heat until sauce thickens. Add oranges and bananas. Heat, but do not cook. Serve over rice. Makes 4 servings.

ALMOND RICE

2 tbs. butter
1/4 cup slivered almonds
1-1/2 cups Minute rice
1-1/3 cups water
1/2 tsp. salt

Melt butter in saucepan and saute almonds until lightly browned. Add rice, water and salt. Bring to boil. Cover and remove from heat. Let stand 5 minutes. Serve with Brazilian Beef. Makes 4 servings.

HERBED STEW WITH MUSHROOM DUMPLINGS

2-1/2 lb. chuck roast
1/4 cup flour
2 tbs. salad oil
1 clove garlic, crushed
1 cup hot water
1 qt. tomato juice
2 tbs. brown sugar
1/2 tsp. dried marjoram
3/4 tsp. dried thyme
3/4 tsp. dried rosemary
6 small onions, quartered
4 carrots, quartered
1 pkg. (10 ozs.) frozen peas
salt and pepper
Mushroom Dumplings, page 45

Cut meat into 1-inch cubes and coat with flour. Heat oil in large kettle. Brown

meat on all sides. Add garlic, water, tomato juice, sugar, and herbs. Cover and simmer 1 hour or until meat is tender. Add onions and carrots. Cook 30 minutes longer. Add peas, salt and pepper. Cook 5 minutes. Reduce heat to low. Drop dumplings by table-spoonfuls on top of stew. Cover and cook 15 minutes. Don't peek. Makes 6 servings.

MUSHROOM DUMPLINGS

1 egg, beaten
2/3 can cream of mushroom soup
1-1/3 cups flour
1 tsp. baking powder

Mix egg with soup. Add flour and baking powder. Mix together well. Cook as directed in Herbed Stew recipe.

BEEF MALAGA

This tangy stew is an interesting combination of sweet and sour.

5 lbs. chuck or round, cubed
paprika
1/4 cup salad oil
2 onions, chopped
1 clove garlic, mashed
1 tsp. oregano
1 tsp. basil

1/2 tsp. thyme
1 cup dry red wine
1 can (10-1/2 ozs.) cream of mushroom soup
2 peaches, mashed
2 cups (1 pt.) sour cream
1/2 lb. grated sharp cheddar cheese
salt and pepper

Dust meat with paprika. Heat oil in Dutch oven. Brown meat on all sides. Drain off fat. Add onions, garlic, oregano, basil, thyme, wine, soup and mashed peaches. Mix well. Cover and bake in a 250°F oven 3 to 4 hours or until meat is tender. Blend in sour cream and cheese. Heat 15 minutes longer. Serve over steamed brown rice. Makes 10 servings.

CHILI CON CARNE

Serve with French bread, green salad and beer.

2 lb. chuck roast
3 tbs. salad oil
1 onion, chopped
2 cloves garlic, minced
1 can (1 lb.) tomatoes
2 cups water
3 tbs. chili powder

2 tbs. cocoa
salt to taste
2 tsp. oregano
1 tsp. cumin
1 tbs. diced green chiles
2 cans (1 lb. ea.) red kidney beans, undrained

Cut meat into 1-inch cubes. Brown in hot oil. Push meat aside. Brown onion and garlic. Stir in tomatoes, water, chili powder, cocoa, salt, oregano, cumin and green chiles. Cover and simmer 1-1/2 hours or until meat is tender. Gently stir in kidney beans. Simmer 15 minutes longer. Makes 4 servings.

GERMAN BEEF STEW

2 lb. chuck roast, cubed
2 tbs. oil
1 large apple
1 large carrot
1 small onion, sliced
1-1/2 cups water
1/3 cup dry red wine
1/2 tsp. anchovy paste
1 clove garlic, minced

2 beef bouillon cubes
1 bay leaf
1/8 tsp. thyme
2 tbs. cornstarch
1/4 cup water
1/4 tsp. Kitchen Bouquet
4 cups cooked noodles
1/4 tsp. poppy seed

Brown meat cubes in hot oil. Peel and shred apple and carrot. Add to meat along with onion, water, wine, anchovy paste, garlic, bouillon, bay leaf and thyme. Cover and cook over low heat 1-1/2 to 2 hours. Add more water as necessary. Remove bay leaf. If thickening is desired, combine cornstarch with water and stir into boiling stew. Add Kitchen Bouquet. Serve over hot noodles. Sprinkle with poppy seed. Makes 4 servings.

IRISH BEEF-STEW PIE

2 lbs. cubed chuck or round
1/3 cup flour
2 tbs. oil
2 cups beef stock
1 cup dry wine
1 tsp. Worcestershire sauce
1 tsp. Kitchen Bouquet
1 clove garlic, minced
1 bay leaf

1 tsp. salt
1/2 tsp. pepper
1/2 tsp. paprika
dash cloves
1 tsp. sugar
4 carrots, cut in chunks
1 can (16 ozs.) boiling onions
1 can (16 ozs.) potatoes
1 (5-1/2 ozs.) pie crust stick

Coat meat with flour and brown on all sides in hot oil. Add the next eleven ingredients. Cover and simmer 1-1/2 hours. Add carrots and cook 20 minutes. Stir in onions and potatoes. Cook until carrots are tender. Make pie crust as directed. Pour stew into large casserole. Cover with crust. Seal edges and slash crust to release steam. Bake in 400°F oven until crust is brown, about 25 minutes. Makes 4 servings.

SHORT RIBS AND DUMPLINGS

3 lbs. beef short ribs
3 tbs. flour
2 tbs. oil
1 pkg. (1-3/8 ozs.) onion soup mix
2 cups water
1 cup dry red wine

1/4 tsp. thyme
1/4 tsp. garlic powder
3 cups sliced carrots
salt and pepper
Dumplings, page 51

Dust ribs with flour. Set remaining flour aside. Heat oil in large saucepan. Add meat and brown well on all sides. Drain off fat. Add reserved flour, soup mix, water, wine, thyme and garlic powder. Cover and simmer 2 hours. Add carrots and cook 45 minutes longer or until meat is done. Prepare dumplings. Skim fat from ribs. Drop dumpling mixture by tablespoonfuls onto simmering stew. Cover and cook 15 minutes without lifting lid. Makes 4 servings.

DUMPLINGS

3/4 cup biscuit mix
1/4 cup corn meal
1 tbs. minced parsley
1 egg
2 tbs. melted butter
1/3 cup milk

Combine biscuit mix, corn meal and parsley. Beat butter and milk together. Add to dry ingredients. Mix until blended. Drop batter by tablespoonfuls onto simmering stew. Cover and cook 15 minutes without lifting the lid. Makes 4 servings.

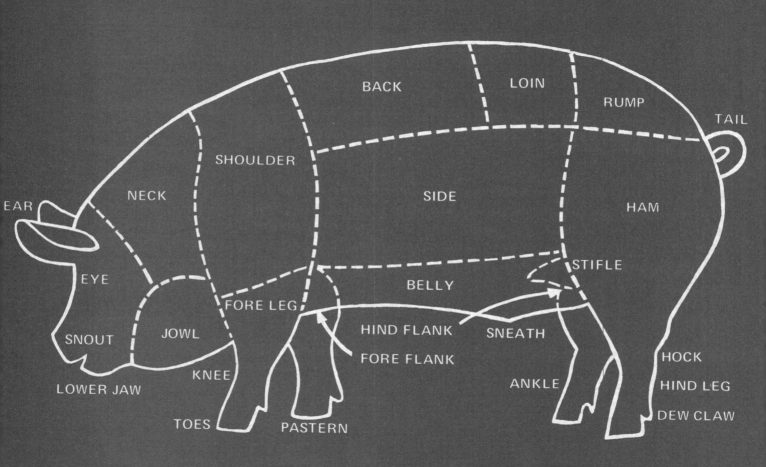

VEAL AND PORK STEWS

OSSO-BUCO

Osso-buco means "bone with a hole." In Milan this world famous dish is served with special tiny spoons for scooping out the delicious marrow. Seafood-cocktail forks work well, too. Serve with Risotto or hot rice or pasta which have been tossed with butter and Parmesan cheese.

3 lbs. veal shank or knuckle with marrow
1 clove garlic, halved
1/4 cup dry sherry
1 onion
2 carrots
1 stalk celery
4 tbs. butter
salt and pepper

1 tbs. flour
1 cup tomato pulp or sauce
1/2 cup dry white wine
1/8 tsp. thyme
1 tbs. minced parsley
chicken stock
1 strip lemon peel, minced
parsley

Cut veal in 2-inch lengths and rub with cut garlic. Brush meat with sherry and let stand at room temperature 30 minutes. Finely chop onion, carrots and celery. Melt 2 tablespoons butter in large saucepan. Add finely chopped vegetables and brown light-

ly. Remove from pan and set aside. Dry meat on paper toweling. Sprinkle with salt and pepper and brown on all sides. Return vegetables to pan. Mix flour and remaining butter to form a roux. Add to meat and vegetables. Stir in tomato pulp, wine, thyme parsley and enough stock to barely cover meat. Cover pan and simmer 1-1/2 hours. Remove cover and simmer 30 minutes. Ten minutes before serving, remove meat from pan. Strain juices. Return meat and strained juices to pan. Heat together thoroughly. To serve, sprinkle meat with lemon peel, salt, pepper and chopped parsley. Makes 4 to 6 servings.

BLANQUETTE DE VEAU

Serve with rice pilaf, glazed carrots and fresh peas.

2 lbs. veal shoulder, cubed
1 veal bone, cracked
1 qt. water
1 onion, quartered
1 carrot, sliced
3 cloves garlic, minced
1/2 tsp. thyme
1 bay leaf
2 tsp. salt
1/2 tsp. sugar

1/2 tsp. white pepper
2 tbs. butter
2 tbs. flour
few grains cayenne pepper
3 egg yolks
2 tbs. lemon juice
1 cup (1/2 pt.) whipping cream
salt and pepper
parsley

Place meat and bone in Dutch oven. Cover with water and bring to a boil. Skim off foam. Add onion, carrot, garlic, thyme, bay leaf, salt, sugar and pepper. Cover and simmer 1-1/2 hours. Remove meat and bones from pot. Place in colander until cool enough to handle. Scoop marrow from bones and set aside. Rinse off meat and discard

fat. Strain stock and rinse out Dutch oven. Return stock and marrow to pot. Turn heat to high and reduce stock to 1-1/2 cups. Melt butter in small saucepan. Stir in flour to make a roux. Remove from heat. Add cayenne and gradually stir in veal stock. Return to heat and cook gently 5 minutes. Mix egg yolks with lemon juice. Blend in cream. Add a little of the hot sauce to egg mixture, beating constantly. Stir back into sauce. Do not let boil or it will separate. Add cooked veal to sauce and gently reheat without boiling. Garnish with fresh parsely. Makes 4 servings.

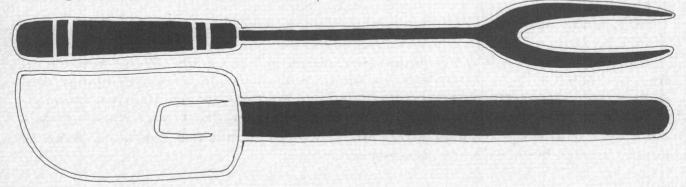

FAR EAST VEAL STEW

2 lbs. cubed veal
2 tsp. Kitchen Bouquet
2 tbs. butter
1 onion, chopped
1/4 lb. mushrooms, sliced
1 cup dry white wine
2 tbs. brown sugar
1/4 cup vinegar
1 tsp. ground ginger

1 tsp. dry mustard
1 tsp. salt
1/4 tsp. pepper
1 can (5 ozs.) water chestnuts
1 tbs. cornstarch
2 tbs. water
2 tbs. red wine
1 cup flaked coconut

Brush veal with Kitchen Bouquet. Heat butter in large skillet. Brown meat on all sides and place in large casserole. Saute onions and mushrooms in pan drippings. Add wine, sugar, vinegar, ginger, mustard, salt and pepper. Pour over meat. Cover casserole and bake in 325°F oven 1-1/2 hours or until meat is tender. Thinly slice chestnuts. Mix cornstarch with water. Add to meat. Stir in wine, coconut and chestnuts. Bake 10 minutes longer. Serve with rice. Makes 4 servings.

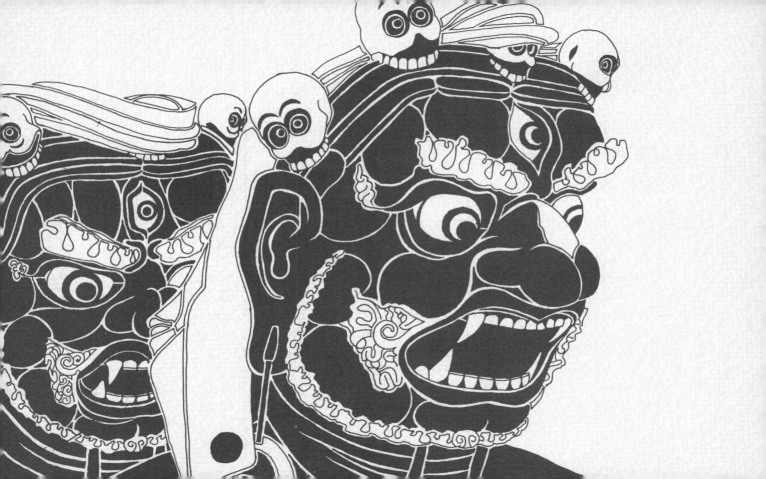

PORK STEW WITH CARAWAY NOODLES

2 lbs. boneless pork shoulder
2 tbs. flour
1 tbs. oil
1/2 cup chopped celery
1/2 green pepper, chopped
1/2 sweet red pepper, chopped
2 cloves garlic, minced

1 chicken bouillon cube
1 can (16 ozs.) green beans
water
1 cup (1/2 pt.) sour cream
salt and pepper
Caraway Noodles, see below
parsley

Trim meat and cut into 1/2 x 2 inch strips. Toss with flour. Heat oil in large skillet. Brown meat. Add celery, green and red pepper and garlic. Cook 3 minutes. Add bouillon cube. Drain beans and combine liquid with enough water to make 1-1/2 cups. Add to pork mixture. Cover and simmer 1 hour or until meat is tender. Stir in beans and sour cream. Season to taste with salt and pepper. Heat to serving temperature. Serve over Caraway noodles. Garnish with parsley. Makes 4 servings.

Caraway Noodles—Cook an 8 ounce package of medium noodles. Drain well and toss with 1/4 cup butter and 1/2 teaspoon caraway seed. Serve with Pork Stew.

HUNGARIAN PORK

Pork lends itself beautifully to Hungarian cooking.

2 lbs. boneless pork
2 tbs. oil
salt and pepper
2 tbs. sweet Hungarian paprika
1 onion, chopped
1 carrot, thinly sliced

1 stalk celery, thinly sliced
1 green pepper, thinly sliced
2 tomatoes, peeled and chopped
1 lb. fresh mushrooms, sliced
1 cup (1/2 pt.) sour cream
1 tbs. flour

Remove all fat from pork and cut into strips. Heat oil in large skillet or electric frying pan. Add pork and brown well on all sides. Add salt, pepper, paprika and onion. Cook 1 minute. Cover and simmer slowly 20 minutes. Add carrot, celery, green pepper and tomatoes. Cover and simmer 1/2 hour. Add mushrooms and cook 10 minutes longer. Combine sour cream and flour. Stir into meat mixture and continue cooking over low heat until thick and creamy. Makes 6 servings.

CHILEAN PORK STEW

Serve in soup plates accompanied by warm, buttered tortillas.

3 lbs. boneless pork
3 tbs. salad oil
2 green peppers, chopped
1 onion, chopped
2 cups chicken stock
1 tsp. salt
pinch cayenne
1/8 tsp. dry mustard

1/2 tsp. Tabasco sauce
2 tsp. brown sugar
1 can (2 lbs.) kidney beans
3 tbs. catsup
1 can (17 ozs.) whole kernel corn, drained
1/2 cup bean liquid
1 tbs. cornstarch
parsley

Trim pork and cut into cubes. Heat oil in large kettle. Brown pork on all sides. Add pepper and onions. Saute until transparent. Stir in stock, salt, cayenne, mustard, Tabasco and brown sugar. Cover and bring to boil. Reduce heat and simmer 1-1/2 hours or until tender. Drain beans, reserving liquid. Add beans to stew along with catsup and corn. Cook 15 minutes. Combine bean liquid and cornstarch. Stir into stew. Cook until thickened. Makes 6 servings.

RIBS AND SAUERKRAUT

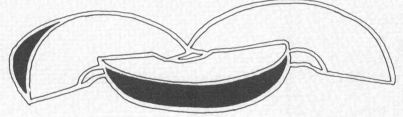

Simple and truly succulent. You'll love these ribs! Serve them with boiled potatoes.

4 lbs. pork spareribs
salt and pepper
1 can (27 ozs.) sauerkraut, drained
2 unpeeled apples, sliced
2 tbs. sugar
2 tsp. caraway seed

Sprinkle ribs with salt and pepper. Brown in Dutch oven or under broiler. Drain off fat. Mix sauerkraut, apples, sugar and caraway seed in Dutch oven. Place ribs meat side up over sauerkraut. Bake, covered, in 300ºF oven 4 hours, or in 325ºF oven 2 hours. Makes 4 servings.

PORK RAGOUT

A combination elegant enough for your best silver and china.

1 Boston pork butt, about 3 lbs.
paprika
2 tbs. salad oil
2 cloves garlic, minced
1 can (10-1/2 ozs.) cream of mushroom soup
1 pkg. (1-3/8 ozs.) dry onion soup mix
1 soup can water

1 soup can dry white wine
1 tsp. Spice Islands Bouquet Garni
1 pkg. (10 ozs.) frozen peas
1 lb. fresh mushrooms, sliced
1 cup (1/2 pt.) sour cream
salt and pepper

Trim fat from meat. Cut meat into 1-1/2 inch cubes. Sprinkle with paprika. Heat oil in Dutch oven. Brown meat on all sides. Add garlic, mushroom soup, onion soup mix, water, wine and Bouquet Garni. Cover and simmer 1-1/2 hours. Cool. Remove all fat as it accumulates on top. Add peas and mushrooms. Cook 5 minutes. Add a little hot sauce to sour cream. Stir warmed sour cream into soup. Season to taste with salt and pepper. Makes 6 servings.

HAM AND BLACK-EYED PEAS

Eating black-eyed peas on New Year's Day is supposed to bring good luck. True or not, you will surely like them prepared this way. Serve with a green salad or relishes and hot, buttered cornbread.

1/2 lb. dry black-eyed peas
4 cups hot water
2 chicken bouillon cubes
1-1/2 lb. ham shank
1 onion, chopped

1 tsp. salt
1/4 tsp. Tabasco
1/2 cup raw rice
1 can (16 ozs.) whole tomatoes, undrained
1/4 cup chopped parsley

Place washed peas in a large kettle. Add water, bouillon cubes, ham shank, onion and Tabasco. Cover and bring to boil. Reduce heat and simmer 1 hour, or until peas are tender. Remove ham shank. When cool enough to handle, remove meat from bone. Return meat to peas. Stir in rice and enough water to just cover rice. Cover and bring to boil. Reduce heat and simmer 20 minutes. Add tomatoes and parsley. Continue cooking 10 minutes. Makes 6 to 8 servings.

LAMB STEWS

LAMB STEW WITH MINT DUMPLINGS

2 lbs. boneless lamb
1 tbs. oil
1 onion, chopped
1 clove garlic, minced
3 cups boiling water
1 cup celery tops
1 tsp. salt
pepper to taste
1/2 tsp. rosemary
6 carrots, peeled
18 small white onions, peeled
1 cup sliced celery
Mint Dumplings, page 69

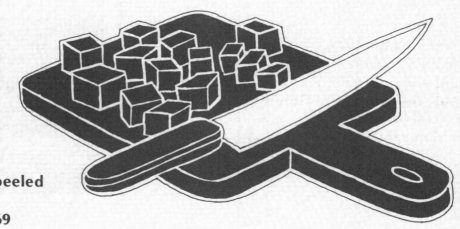

Trim fat from lamb and cut into 1-1/2 inch cubes. Heat oil in Dutch oven. Brown meat a few pieces at a time. Remove from pot and set aside. Add onion and garlic. Saute until golden, adding more oil if necessary. Add boiling water, meat, celery tops,

salt and rosemary. Cover and simmer 1 hour or until meat is tender. Remove celery tops. Cut carrots into 1-inch pieces. Arrange carrots, onions and celery around meat. Cover and simmer 30 minutes or until vegetables are tender. Drop dumplings by tablespoonfuls on top of simmering stew. Cook, uncovered, 10 minutes. Cover and cook 10 minutes longer. Makes 4 servings.

MINT DUMPLINGS

2 cups biscuit mix
2 tbs. chopped fresh mint
3/4 cup milk
1 tsp. mint jelly

Combine biscuit mix and mint in mixing bowl. Add milk and jelly. Mix until moistened. Drop by tablespoonfuls onto simmering stew. Cook, uncovered, 10 minutes. Cover and cook 10 minutes longer. Makes 4 servings.

IRISH STEW

A combination bound to bring out the "blarney" in you!

3 lbs. boneless lamb
2 tbs. oil
salt and pepper
3 cups water
1/2 lb. small turnips
4 carrots, sliced

2 onions, quartered
4 potatoes, quartered
1 clove garlic, crushed
2 tbs. flour
1/4 cup water
2 tsp. Worcestershire sauce

Cut lamb into 1-1/2 inch cubes. Heat oil in Dutch oven. Brown lamb on all sides. Add salt and pepper. Stir in water. Boil 2 minutes. Reduce heat. Cover and simmer 1 hour. Cut turnips into 1/2-inch slices. Add to meat along with carrots, onions, potatoes and garlic. Bring to boil, then reduce heat to simmer. Cover and cook 45 minutes. Combine flour, water and Worcestershire. Add to stew, stirring constantly until smooth and thickened. Makes 6 servings.

RUSSIAN LAMB STEW

Simple to assemble and pretty to serve.

1/4 cup butter
2-1/2 lbs. lamb neck or shoulder
1 tsp. paprika
1 onion, thinly sliced
1 can (8 ozs.) tomato sauce
1 cup beef stock
salt and pepper
1 tsp. Spice Islands Bouquet Garni

1/2 tsp. crushed rosemary
1 clove garlic, crushed
5 medium potatoes, peeled and quartered
1/2 lb. mushrooms, thickly sliced
1 pkg. (10 ozs.) frozen peas
1 cup (1/2 pt.) sour cream
parsley

Melt butter in large saucepan. Add lamb, paprika and onion. Cook until browned. Add tomato sauce, stock, salt and pepper, bouquet garni, rosemary, garlic and potatoes. Boil 2 minutes. Lower heat. Cover and simmer 1 hour. Add mushrooms and peas. Simmer 20 to 30 minutes. Stir in sour cream. Heat gently without boiling. Garnish with parsley. Makes 4 to 6 servings.

LAMB CURRY

It is traditional for curry to be accompanied by small dishes of condiments and rice. Pappadums, cracker-like bread, serve as excellent pushers for the rice. They become crisp and puffy when fried. Pappadums can be found in speciality food shops.

3 lbs. boneless lamb
3 tbs. peanut oil
3 onions, chopped
2 bay leaves
2 cloves garlic, minced
1/8 tsp. thyme
4 to 6 tbs. Madras curry powder

1 qt. chicken stock
salt and pepper
1 apple, peeled and chopped
3 tbs. cornstarch
1/2 cup half-and-half
condiments

Trim and cube lamb. Heat oil in large kettle. Brown lamb and onions. Drain off fat. Add bay leaves, garlic, thyme, curry powder and stock. Cover and simmer 1-1/2 hours or until tender. Season with salt and pepper. Add apple. Combine cornstarch with cream and stir into sauce. Cook until thickened. Serve with rice and condiments. Makes 6 servings.

Condiments:

Major Gray's chutney
chopped peanuts
shredded coconut
raisins
crumbled crisp bacon
minced green onions
sliced bananas
chopped hard-cooked eggs

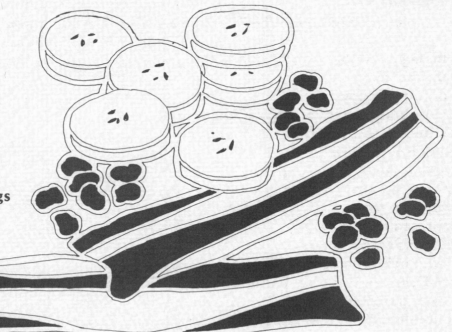

LAMB A LA BOMBAY

A favorite served at the "Casa de los Ninos" in Sacramento, California.

3 lb. leg of lamb
3 tbs. butter
1 onion, chopped
4 cups boiling beef broth
2 cloves garlic, minced
1-1/2 tsp. tumeric
1/2 tsp. salt
1/4 tsp. cumin
1/2 tsp. ginger
2 tbs. lemon juice
1/2 cups raisins
1/4 cup chopped green pepper
2 red unpeeled apples, chopped
steamed rice
condiments*

Remove fat from leg of lamb and cut into chunks. Heat butter in large kettle or Dutch oven. Brown onions and remove from pan. Add lamb and brown well on all sides. Add broth, garlic, tumeric, salt, cumin, ginger, lemon juice, raisins and green pepper. Simmer, uncovered, 25 minutes. Add apples. Cover and simmer 20 minutes. Serve over rice with condiments. Makes 6 to 8 servings.

*Shredded coconut, chopped green onions, chopped hard-cooked eggs, chopped salted peanuts, crumbled cooked bacon, chutney.

LAMB AVGOLEMONO

3 lbs. boneless lamb
2 bunches celery
2 tbs. olive oil
1 bunch green onions, chopped
2 onions, chopped
2 cups water

fresh dill, chopped
2 tbs. chopped parsley
salt and pepper
3 eggs
2 tbs. flour
juice of 1-1/2 lemons

Trim lamb and cut into 2-inch cubes. Cut celery into 1-1/2 inch pieces. Heat oil in large kettle. Saute onions until transparent. Add lamb and brown on all sides. Stir in water, dill, parsley, salt, pepper and celery. Bring mixture to boil. Cover and simmer 1-1/2 hours, or until meat is tender. Remove from heat and allow to cool while preparing sauce. Beat eggs until light. Add flour and lemon juice. Mix well. Ladle in a little of the hot liquid from stew, stirring occasionally, until about 1 cup of hot liquid has been added. Slowly pour sauce into stew. Heat gently and serve immediately. Makes 6 servings.

MALAYSIAN LAMB

Serve with steamed rice and a chilled green salad.

2 lbs. lamb stewing meat	1 tbs. minced fresh ginger
1 tbs. vinegar	1 clove garlic, mashed
1 tsp. chili powder	1/16 to 1/8 tsp. saffron
1 tsp. salt	salt to taste
1 tbs. salad oil	1 can (1 lb.) whole tomatoes
1 tbs. sesame oil	1 tbs. chopped fresh Chinese parsley or cilantro
2 onions, sliced	Chinese parsley or cilantro
1 can (4 ozs.) diced green chiles	1 cup (1/2 pt.) plain yogurt

Cut lamb into 1-inch pieces. Coat with vinegar, salt and chili powder. Marinate 15 minutes. Heat oil in large skillet or electric frying pan. Add lamb and brown on all sides. Remove from pan. Add onions, chiles, ginger, garlic, saffron and salt. Saute 5 minutes or until onions are soft. Add tomatoes and lamb. Cover and simmer 1/2 hour, or until meat is tender. Add chopped cilantro and yogurt. Simmer 5 minutes longer. Makes 4 servings.

COMBINATION AND GAME STEWS

SPANISH PAELLA

3 lb. chicken, cut up
1/4 cup olive oil
1 cup chopped onion
3 cloves garlic, crushed
2-1/2 cups rice
1 qt. chicken stock
1/2 tsp. powdered saffron
salt and pepper to taste

1/2 tsp. <u>each</u> tarragon, paprika
1 tsp. crushed oregano
1 pkg. (7 ozs.) frozen artichoke hearts
3 pepperonis, sliced
16 fresh clams, well scrubbed
1 lb. raw shrimp
1 pkg. (10 ozs.) frozen peas
1 jar (3 ozs.) pimientos

Wash and dry chicken. Heat oil in Dutch oven. Brown chicken. Remove from pan and set aside. Add onion and garlic to Dutch oven. Brown and remove. Add rice to oil (add more oil if necessary). Cook, stirring, 5 minutes until golden. In a separate pan, heat stock with saffron, pepper, salt, tarragon, paprika and oregano. Stir hot stock into rice. Add artichoke hearts, pepperonis, chicken and onions. Toss peas into mixture. Poke clams and shrimp down into the paella. Cover. Bake in 350°F oven for 1 hour. Decorate top with pimientos. Makes 8 servings.

QUICK ITALIAN STEW

Here's a family favorite that doesn't need a great deal of cooking time.

1 lb. Italian sausages
1 lb. ground beef
2 tsp. Kitchen Bouquet
2 cans (1 lb. ea.) stewed tomatoes
1 tsp. Italian seasoning
2 cans (1 lb. ea.) whole potatoes, drained

1 pkg. (10 ozs.) frozen Italian green beans
3 tbs. flour
3 tbs. water
salt and pepper
Parmesan cheese

Slice sausages 1-inch thick and brown in electric frying pan or large skillet. Mix ground beef with Kitchen Bouquet and shape into meatballs. Push sausage to one side of pan and brown meatballs. Drain off all fat. Add tomatoes, Italian seasoning, potatoes and beans. Cover and simmer 10 minutes. Blend flour with water and stir into stew. Cover and cook 10 minutes longer or until beans are tender. Salt and pepper to taste. Garnish with grated Prmesan if desired. Makes 4-6 servings.

CHOUCROUTE GARNIE

The Alsatians originated this famous dish. Accompany it with boiled, parsleyed potatoes, good mustard and beer.

6 cups sauerkraut
1/2 lb. bacon slices
2 carrots, sliced
2 onions, chopped
1 clove garlic, minced
6 juniper berries, crushed
8 peppercorns, coarsley ground
6 smoked pork chops
1-1/2 lbs. ham, sliced
6 bratwurst, browned
2 cups chicken stock
1 jigger gin
1 cup dry white wine
6 frankfurters

Wash sauerkraut in several changes of cold water. Place in colander and press out all liquid. Drain on paper toweling. Line bottom of a large, round pot with heavy lid, with half of the bacon slices. Place carrots, onions and garlic on top of bacon. Layer sauerkraut 1-inch thick. Press lightly and sprinkle with juniper berries and freshly ground pepper. Then alternate layers of pork chops, ham and bratwurst with layers of sauerkraut. End with a layer of sauerkraut on top. Leave 2 inches of space at top of pot. Add stock, gin and wine. Place remaining bacon slices on top. Cover tightly and bake in 350°F oven 2 hours. Remove from oven and bury frankfurters under sauerkraut. Bake uncovered 1/2 hour longer. To serve, arrange sauerkraut on large platter and place meat and sausages on top. Makes 6 servings.

This dish can be made in advance and refrigerated. Bring to room temperature, then bake in 305°F oven 1/2 hour or until thoroughly heated.

COLOMBIAN PASTELADO

3 tbs. salad oil
6 chicken pieces, skinned
6 small pork chops
1 qt. water
2 cups raw rice
2 tbs. butter
3 carrots, diced
2 onions, chopped
3 cloves garlic, minced

1 can (16 ozs.) whole kernel corn
1 pkg. (10 ozs.) frozen peas
4 pimientos, chopped
24 stuffed green olives
1 bottle (2 ozs.) capers and
    half the liquid
2 tsp. salt
1 tsp. pepper

Heat oil in large kettle. Brown chicken and chops. Drain off fat. Pour water over meat. Cover and simmer 45 minutes or until tender. Remove chicken and chops and place in large casserole. Measure 3 cups of the stock. Cook rice in stock 20 to 25 minutes. Melt butter and gently saute carrots, onions and garlic until tender. Drain corn, add to rice along with peas, pimiento, olives, capers and liquid, salt and pepper. Spoon rice mixture over meat. Cover and bake slowly in a 225°F oven at least 1 hour.

84

SCOTTISH HOT POT

1 lb. cubed chuck or round steak
3 tbs. flour
4 potatoes
2 apples
1 onion
1/2 lb. pork link sausages
salt and pepper
2 cups tomato juice
3 beef bouillon cubes
pinch of sage

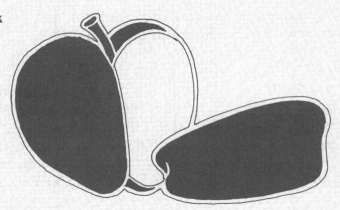

Dredge meat cubes in flour. Peel potatoes, apples and onions. Slice each 1/4-inch thick. Arrange half of potatoes, apples and onions in bottom of a 2-quart casserole. Add meat and sausages, then remaining potatoes, apples and onions. Sprinkle each layer with salt and pepper. Heat tomato juice with bouillon cubes. Add sage. Pour over ingredients in casserole. Cover and bake in 350ºF oven 1-1/2 to 2 hours. Stir and serve. Makes 4 servings.

HUNGARIAN GOULASH

Goulash can be many mixtures, but goulash from Hungary makes its distinction with the generous use of sweet Hungarian paprika.

1/4 cup flour
1 tsp. seasoned salt
1/4 tsp. pepper
1-1/2 lb. chuck roast, cubed
1 lb. pork or veal, cubed
3 tbs. oil
2 cups beef broth

2 onions, sliced
2 cloves garlic, minced
4 potatoes, peeled and quartered
1 cup (1/2 pt.) sour cream
1 tbs. sweet Hungarian paprika
1 tsp. Worcestershire sauce
2 tbs. chopped parsley

Combine flour, salt and pepper. Coat meat with flour. Heat oil in large kettle. Brown meat well. Stir in broth. Cover and simmer 1 hour. Add onion, garlic and potatoes. Bring to boil and simmer 30 to 40 minutes or until potatoes are tender. Combine sour cream, paprika, Worcestershire and parsley. Stir into meat mixture. Simmer gently 10 minutes. Makes 6 to 8 servings.

VENISON STEW

1/4 cup flour
1 tsp. salt
few grains cayenne
dash thyme, nutmeg and cloves
3 lb. deer or elk steak
2 tbs. oil
3 onions, sliced
2 tomatoes, peeled and quartered

1-1/2 tbs. Worcestershire sauce
1-1/2 cups Burgundy wine
1 clove garlic, minced
1 tsp. Spice Islands Bouquet Garni
salt and pepper
1/2 lb. mushrooms, sauteed in butter
cooked rice
current jelly

Sift flour and seasonings together. Pound seasoned flour into steak and cut into 1-inch cubes. Heat oil in Dutch oven. Sear meat on all sides. Add onions and saute until brown. Add tomatoes, Worcestershire, wine, garlic and Bouquet Garni. Cover and bake in 350°F oven 2-1/2 hours. Add salt and pepper. Refrigerate overnight. When ready to serve, bring stew to a boil. Reduce heat and add sauteed mushrooms. Stir until thoroughly heated. Serve with rice and current jelly. Makes 6 servings.

BEAR STEW

4–5 lbs. bear meat, cubed
water
1/4 cup oil
1 onion, chopped
1 clove garlic, minced
2 small hot peppers
1/2 tsp. rosemary
3 drops Tabasco sauce
salt and pepper
3/4 cup dry sherry

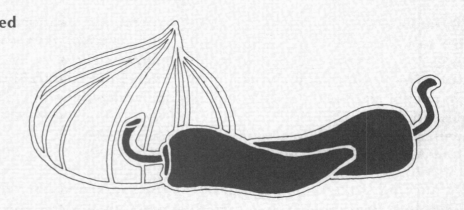

Place meat in large kettle. Cover with water and bring to a boil. Remove from heat. Drain and rinse meat thoroughly. Dry on paper toweling. Heat oil and slowly brown meat on all sides. Add onions, garlic, peppers, rosemary, Tabasco, salt and pepper. Cook 30 minutes. Stir in sherry and cook slowly until absorbed into meat. Add water to cover meat and simmer until tender. Makes 6 servings.

INDEX

90

Beautiful soup, so rich and green,
Waiting in a hot tureen!
Who for such dainties would not stoop?
Soup of the evening, beautiful soup!
    Beau-ootiful Soo-oop!
    Beau-ootiful Soo-oop!
Soo-oop of the e-e-evening,
    Beautiful, beautiful soup!

from Alice in Wonderland
by Lewis Carroll

books designed with giving in mind

Kid's Pets Book
Make It Ahead
French Cooking
Soups & Stews
Crepes & Omelets
Microwave Cooking
Vegetable Cookbook
Kid's Arts and Crafts
Bread Baking
The Crockery Pot Cookbook
Kid's Garden Book
Classic Greek Cooking

The Compleat American
Housewife 1776
Low Carbohydrate Cookbook
Kid's Cookbook
Italian
Cheese Guide & Cookbook
Miller's German
Quiche & Souffle
To My Daughter, With Love
Natural Foods
Chinese Vegetarian
Jewish Gourmet
Working Couples

Mexican
Sunday Breakfast
Fisherman's Wharf Cookbook
Charcoal Cookbook
Ice Cream Cookbook
Hippo Hamburger
Blender Cookbook
The Wok, a Chinese Cookbook
Cast Iron Cookbook
Japanese Country
Fondue Cookbook
Food Processor Cookbook
Peanuts & Popcorn

from nitty gritty productions

To Michael and Terry

SOUPS

& Stews

by
Joanne Waring Lindeman

Illustrated by Mike Nelson

© Copyright 1976
Nitty Gritty Productions
Concord, California

A Nitty Gritty Book*
Published by
Nitty Gritty Productions
P.O. Box 5457
Concord, California 94524

*Nitty Gritty Books — Trademark
Owned by Nitty Gritty Productions
Concord, California

ISBN O-911954-37-6

Library of Congress Cataloging in Publication Data

Lindeman, Joanne Waring.
  Soups & stews.

  Consists of 2 pts., Soups & stews and Stews &
soups, inverted with respect to each other.
  Includes indexes.
  1. Soups. 2. Stews. I. Title. II. Title:
Stews & soups.
TX757.L56   641.8'13   76-27363
ISBN 0-911954-37-6

TABLE OF CONTENTS

INTRODUCTION

The first soups were made in stockpots which were kept on the stove continuously. Vegetables and scraps of meat were tossed into the pot and the constantly changing soup was served at every meal. Ingredients used were those common to the region, and often the resulting soup became a tradition and was passed down from generation to generation. Italian minestrone and Russian borsch are good examples.

Today, soups are no longer the mainstay of our diets, but they are still popular. Many a cook's reputation has been built on good soup.

There is no mystery to homemade soups, and although the cooking process takes time, it requires little attention. Vegetables and herbs from the garden can be used during the growing season and with the help of a home freezer, the resulting soup can be served months later.

Always a treat at lunch, soups are also delicious and nutritious for dinner, either as a separate course or as a one-dish meal, and there is an ever increasing number of soup-for-breakfast fans.

When time is not available for a slowly cooked recipe, the creative cook can use canned and packaged soups as a base for "quickie soups." I have included several of these in one section of this book so you can see how a few fresh ingredients can

1

enhance the canned or dried product and give it a "homemade" touch.

Soup tureens add a glamorous element to soup presentations and you can preheat the tureen with boiling water for hot soups or chill it in the freezer for cold soups. A variety of soup bowls are available. Use dainty bowls for cream soup and clear broth, and heavy earthenware bowls for hearty soups, to match the "personality" of the soup to the bowl.

Salt is important, but it is best to allow the soup to cook for a while before adding it. Some ingredients contain salt and long cooking concentrates the liquid so less salt is required as cooking proceeds. If you do add too much salt, the addition of a large raw potato will often save the day.

There are many delightful soup accompaniments and here is a special one I thought you might enjoy. My 7 year old son, Michael, made pretzels at school the other day. Besides being good for munching, they went extremely well with soup. They are fun and easy, and children love making them.

FAT PRETZELS

1 pkg. active dry yeast
1-1/2 cups warm water
1 tsp. salt
1 tbs. sugar

4 cups flour
1 large egg, beaten
coarse salt

   Dissolve yeast in warm water. Add salt and sugar. Blend in flour and knead dough until smooth. As soon as dough is kneaded, cut into small pieces and roll into ropes. Twist ropes into pretzel shapes. Place on foil-lined cookie sheets. Brush pretzels with beaten egg and sprinkle with coarse salt. Bake in 425°F oven 12 to 15 minutes until brown.

   I hope this collection of recipes will stimulate your taste buds and inspire you to serve soup often.

Jeanne Lindeman

3

CHILLED SOUPS

CREAM OF AVOCADO

This soup is the perfect choice for a hot day, but delightful anytime of year. It will be one of your favorites and it is so easy to make.

2 ripe avocados
1-1/2 cups chicken broth
3 tbs. lemon juice
1 cup light cream
salt and pepper
dash Tabasco
Bacos or croutons

Peel and seed avocados. Dice pulp and place in blender container. Add chicken broth and lemon juice. Cover and blend until smooth. Add cream, salt, pepper and Tabasco. Blend well. Chill. Serve icy cold topped with Bacos or croutons. Makes 4 servings.

CREAMY GAZPACHO

1 lb. ripe tomatoes
1/2 large cucumber
1/2 cup soft bread crumbs
1 clove garlic, mashed
1 tbs. salad oil
1 tbs. vinegar
2 cups cold water
salt and pepper
1 tsp. McCormick's Season All
dash Tabsco
1 cup (1/2 pt.) heavy cream
finely chopped parsley

Peel and chop tomatoes and cucumber. Put into blender container along with bread crumbs, garlic, oil, vinegar and water. Cover and blend 2 minutes. Chill mixture until icy cold. When ready to serve, stir in salt, pepper, Season All, Tabasco and cream. Serve in chilled bowls garnished with finely chopped parsley. Makes 4 servings.

CURRIED CUCUMBER SOUP

Also delicious served hot as the first course of a light meal.

2 cups peeled diced cucumber
1/2 onion, chopped
1/2 cup peeled finely diced potatoes
2 tbs. chopped parsley
2 cups chicken stock
Accent
1/2 tsp. dry mustard
1 tsp. curry powder
1/8 tsp. minced garlic
salt and pepper
1/3 cup heavy cream

Combine all ingredients, except cream, in a saucepan. Cover and simmer 30 minutes or until vegetables are tender. Force mixture through a sieve to make it smooth. Stir in cream. Chill. Serve garnished with sour cream. Makes 2 to 4 servings.

8

CHILLED SPINACH SOUP

1 pkg. (10 oz.) frozen chopped spinach
3 tbs. butter
1 small onion, finely chopped
3 tbs. flour
2 chicken bouillon cubes
3-1/2 cups milk
salt and pepper
nutmeg
croutons and sour cream

Cook spinach according to package directions. Drain thoroughly. Melt butter in saucepan. Add onion and saute until transparent. Stir in flour and bouillon cubes. Gradually blend in milk. Continue stirring until soup thickens and comes to a boil. Add seasonings and well drained spinach. Chill several hours. Serve in individual bowls topped with a dash of nutmeg, croutons and a dollop of sour cream. Also good served hot. Makes 4 servings.

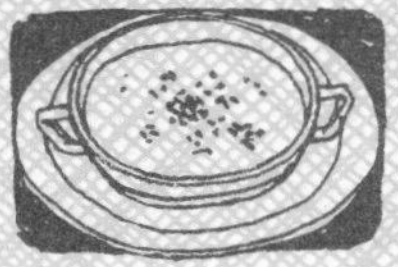

GAZPACHO

This Spanish tradition is first cousin to a salad but even more refreshing. It must be served icy cold.

4 cups tomato juice
2 beef bouillon cubes
2 tomatoes
1/2 cup chopped, unpeeled cucumbers
1/4 cup chopped green pepper
1/4 cup chopped onion

1/4 cup wine vinegar
2 tbs. salad oil
1 tsp. salt
1 tsp. Worcestershire sauce
6 drops Tabasco

Bring tomato juice to boiling. Add bouillon cubes and stir until dissolved. Remove from heat and cool. Peel, seed and dice tomatoes. Add to cooled broth along with remaining ingredients. Refrigerate. Serve in chilled bowls. Makes 8 servings.

BUTTERMILK SEAFOOD SOUP

To be at its best, this soup must chill for several hours.

2 green onions
1/2 lb. green peppers, minced
1 small cucumber, peeled and diced
1 tsp. dried tarragon, crushed
1 tsp. salt
1 tsp. Dijon mustard
1/2 tsp. sugar

2 tsp. Worcestershire sauce
dash Tabasco
1 qt. buttermilk
3 cups milk
8 ozs. fresh crabmeat, flaked
1-1/2 cups small cooked shrimp
lemon pepper

Thinly slice onions. Chop tops and set aside. Combine onion slices, green pepper, cucumber, tarragon, salt, mustard, sugar, Worcestershire and Tabasco in large bowl or soup tureen. Add buttermilk, milk, crab and shrimp. Stir to blend. Chill at least 3 hours or overnight. Stir before serving and garnish with chopped green onion tops and lemon pepper. Makes 6 to 8 servings.

CREAM SOUPS AND BISQUES

CREAM OF FRESH ASPARAGUS SOUP

1-1/2 lbs. fresh asparagus, trimmed
4 green onions
1 qt. chicken stock
2 fresh spinach leaves
1/2 tsp. lemon juice
1/4 tsp. dried tarragon
1 tsp. chopped parsley
1/8 tsp. coriander
salt and pepper
2 tbs. butter
1 tbs. flour
1 cup (1/2 pt.) half-and-half
1 egg yolk
mace or nutmeg

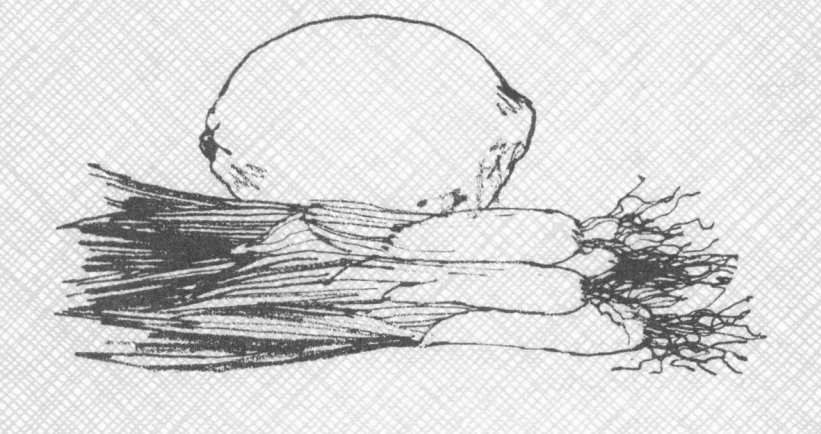

Cut 2-inch tips from asparagus. Cut remaining spears into small pieces. Slice onions, tops included, and set aside. Steam asparagus tips in a small amount of water

14

until tender, about 7 minutes. Drain and set aside. Heat stock. Add spinach leaves, lemon juice, tarragon, parsley, coriander and cut-up asparagus spears. Simmer 1/2 hour. Remove asparagus. Add salt and pepper to taste. Melt butter in skillet. Saute sliced onions until golden. Sprinkle in flour and stir well. Add asparagus and cook 5 minutes. Scrape bits from pan and add with onion mixture to boiling stock. Simmer 10 minutes. Cool slightly. Pour mixture into blender container. Cover and blend until smooth. Pour into saucepan and place over low heat. Combine half-and-half with egg yolks. Stir into soup. Add asparagus tips. Heat but do not boil. Sprinkle lightly with mace or nutmeg. Makes 4 to 6 servings.

15

CREAM OF ARTICHOKE SOUP

A delicate soup, garnished with thin lemon slices.

1 can (12 ozs.) artichoke hearts
1 can (13-3/4 ozs.) chicken broth
1 tsp. lemon juice
1/2 tsp. onion powder
1/2 tsp. salt
pepper to taste
1 cup (1/2 pt.) whipping cream
6 thin lemon slices

Rinse and drain artichoke hearts. Place in blender container with chicken broth. Cover and blend on high speed 1 minute. Pour mixture into saucepan with lemon juice, onion powder, salt and pepper. Bring to boil. Remove from heat and add cream. Adjust salt and pepper. Reheat slowly, and do not let boil. Float 1 lemon slice on each serving. Makes 6 servings.

LEEK AND POTATO SOUP

Serve this soup icy cold and you'll have a delicious vichyssoise

4 bunches leeks	2 cups (1 pt.) whipping cream
1/2 cup (1/4 lb.) butter	2 tbs. sour cream
4 medium potatoes, thinly sliced	salt, pepper and nutmeg
1 stalk celery, minced	2 tbs. sherry
1 tbs. chopped parsley	2 tsp. Worcestershire sauce
2 qts. chicken stock	chopped chives

Thoroughly wash leeks. Slice white parts only. Melt butter in large saucepan. Add leeks and saute until soft but not browned. Add potatoes, celery, parsley and chicken stock. Simmer 30 minutes. Cool. Put mixture through a sieve or in blender. Return to saucepan. Add cream, sour cream, salt, pepper, nutmeg, wine and Worcestershire. Heat, but do not boil. Serve garnished with chopped chives. Makes 8 to 10 servings.

LETTUCE SOUP WITH SESAME CROUTONS

As with all cream soups, heat just to the serving temperature.

1/4 cup butter
3 green onions, minced
1/4 cup flour
2 cups chicken stock
1 tsp. lemon juice
5 cups (packed) shredded lettuce
1 cup milk
1 cup half-and-half
salt and white pepper

Heat butter in saucepan. Saute onions until tender but not browned. Stir in flour. Gradually add broth and cook, stirring, until thickened and smooth. Add lemon juice and lettuce. Cover and simmer 5 minutes. Add milk, half-and-half, salt and pepper. Heat and serve with Sesame Croutons. Makes 6 servings.

SESAME CROUTONS

2 tbs. oil
2 cups bread cubes (1/2-in.)
1 tbs. sesame seed
salt

    Heat oil in skillet. Add bread cubes. Stir over medium heat 3 minutes, or until crisp. Sprinkle with sesame seed and salt. Brown 1 minute longer.

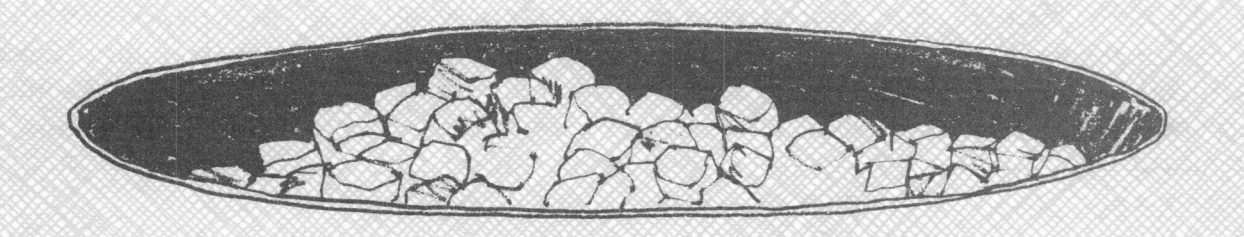

CREAM OF MUSHROOM SOUP

1 lb. mushrooms
1 bunch green onions
2 tbs. butter
salt and pepper
2 cans (10-1/2 ozs. ea.) beef broth
1 can water
1/2 cup dry white wine
1 cup whipping cream
2 egg yolks

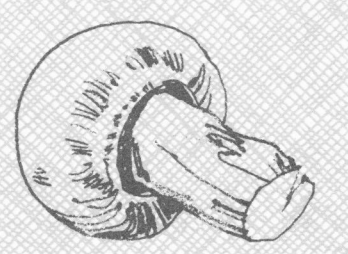

Finely chop mushrooms and onions (use blender on "chop" setting, if available). Melt butter in large saucepan. Add mushroom mixture and saute until tender. Season with salt and pepper. Add broth, water and wine. Simmer, covered, 1 hour. Combine cream and egg yolks. Slowly blend in about 1/4 cup of the hot soup. Stir egg mixture back into pot of soup. Bring to serving temperature. Do not allow to boil. Makes 6 servings.

MUSHROOM BISQUE

1/4 cup butter
1 lb. mushrooms, finely chopped
3 shallots, minced
1/4 cup flour
1/2 tsp. salt
dash of cayenne
1 cup chicken broth
3 cups milk
1 tbs. dry sherry or lemon juice
salt and pepper
lemon slices and parsley

Melt butter in saucepan. Cook mushrooms and shallots until tender, about 10 minutes. Add flour, salt and cayenne. Gradually stir in broth and milk. Cook, stirring, 5 minutes. Add sherry or lemon juice and salt and pepper to taste. Garnish with lemon slices and parsley. Makes 4 servings.

PUMPKIN SOUP

3 tbs. butter
1/2 cup chopped green onion
2 cups (1 lb. can) mashed pumpkin
2 cups chicken stock
1 tsp. Spice Islands Beau Monde Seasoning
salt and pepper
1 cup half-and-half

Heat butter in saucepan. Saute onion until tender but not browned. Add pumpkin, chicken broth, Beau Monde, salt and pepper. Bring to a boil. Cover and simmer 15 minutes. Pour into blender container. Cover and blend until smooth. Return to saucepan. Stir in half-and-half. Bring to serving temperature over low heat. Makes 4 to 6 servings.

CREAM OF SUMMER SQUASH SOUP

Serve this unusual soup with grilled cheese sandwiches for a great luncheon treat.

1 lb. zucchini or yellow crookneck squash
2 tbs. butter
2 tbs. chopped shallots
2 tbs. water
1/2 tsp. curry powder
1 can (13-3/4 ozs.) chicken broth
1/2 cup heavy cream
salt and white pepper

Thinly slice squash. Heat butter in large saucepan. Add squash, shallots and water. Cover and simmer gently 10 minutes. Do not let squash brown. Cool. Transfer mixture to blender container. Add remaining ingredients. Cover and blend until smooth. Return to saucepan and heat slowly to serving temperature. Makes 4 servings.

CREAM OF FRESH TOMATO SOUP

8 large tomatoes
1/4 cup butter
2 tbs. oil
1 onion, sliced
2 tbs. chopped fresh dill
salt and pepper

1/4 cup flour
3-1/2 cups chicken stock
1 cup (1/2 pt.) whipping cream
1/2 tsp. sugar
2 tbs. butter
Baked Bread Slices, page 49

Peel, seed and chop tomatoes. Set aside. Heat butter and oil in large kettle. Add onion, dill, salt and pepper. Cook over low heat until onions are soft. Add tomatoes. Cover and simmer 15 minutes. Blend flour with 1/2 cup chicken stock. Stir into tomato mixture. Add remaining stock and simmer 5 minutes, stirring constantly. Cool. Pour mixture into blender container. Cover and blend until smooth. Return soup to saucepan. Add cream and sugar. Stir over low heat until hot and well blended. Add 2 tablespoons butter. Stir until melted. Serve garnished with Baked Bread Slices or croutons. Also delicious served icy cold. Makes 6 to 8 servings.

BEST OYSTER STEW

1 pt. small fresh oysters
3 tbs. butter
1/4 cup minced onion
1 clove garlic, crushed
1 stalk celery, minced
1 tsp. Spice Islands Beau Monde
dash mace

1 cup whole milk
1 cup sour cream
1 cup light cream
salt and lemon-pepper
parsley for garnish
oyster crackers

Drain oysters, reserving liquid. (If oysters are large, cut in half.) Melt butter in large saucepan. Saute onion, garlic and celery 5 minutes or until onion is transparent. Add oysters and Beau Monde Seasoning. Cook until oyster edges curl. Add oyster liquid and a dash of mace. Simmer over low heat 5 minutes. Stir in milk. Graduallly add sour cream, stirring until smooth. Add light cream. Heat, but do not boil. Season with salt and lemon-pepper. Serve in heated bowls. Garnish with parsley and pass oyster crackers. Makes 4 servings.

SHRIMP BISQUE

1 lb. large raw shrimp
1/4 cup butter
1 small onion, finely chopped
1/2 cup diced celery
2 tbs. flour
1 qt. milk
salt to taste
1/2 tsp. each Tabasco and paprika
3 tsp. lemon juice
lemon pepper, paprika

Devein and coarsely chop shrimp. Melt butter in large saucepan. Add onion and celery. Cook until onion is transparent but not brown. Add shrimp and cook 2 minutes, stirring frequently. Stir in flour. Gradually add milk, salt, Tabasco, paprika and lemon juice. Bring to a boil. Reduce heat and simmer 5 minutes. Serve immediately garnished with lemon pepper and paprika. Makes 4 to 6 servings.

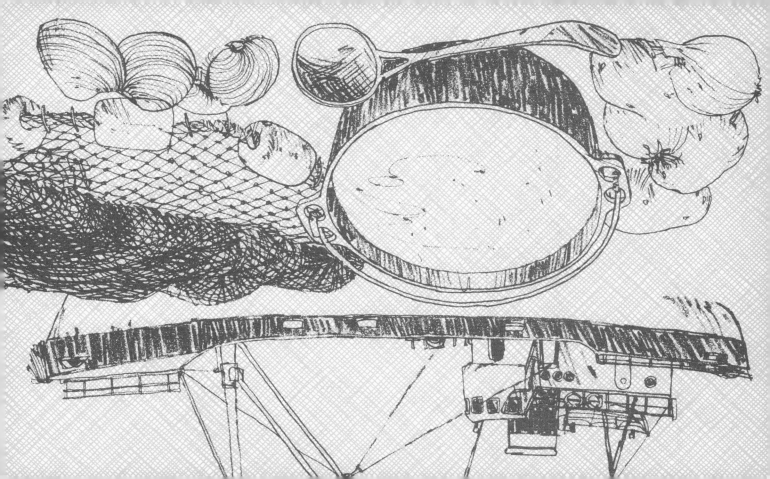

CHOWDERS

TYROLEAN CABBAGE CHOWDER

Serve with pumpernickel bread and sausages for an outstanding meal.

3 tbs. butter
1/2 lb. cabbage, shredded
1 large potato, grated
2 cups milk
1 cup water
salt and pepper
1/4 lb. Swiss cheese, grated

Melt 2 tablespoons butter in a large saucepan. Add cabbage and potato. Simmer slowly until vegetables are soft. Mash with a fork. Gradually blend in milk and water. Add remaining butter. Cover and simmer gently 15 minutes. Add seasonings to taste. Stir in cheese until melted. Makes 4 servings.

SPINACH CHOWDER WITH CHEESE STRAWS

1 pkg. (10 ozs.) frozen chopped spinach
2 cans (13 ozs. ea.) vichyssoise
1 cup milk
2 tsp. granulated chicken bouillon
1 tbs. instant minced onion
4 hard-cooked eggs, sliced

Combine spinach, vichyssoise, milk, bouillon and onion in a large saucepan. Heat slowly about 20 minutes, or until spinach is thawed. Stir occasionally. Cover and simmer 5 minutes. Ladle into soup bowls and garnish with egg slices. Makes 4 to 6 servings.

Flaky Cheese Straws—Defrost a 10 ounce package of frozen patty shells. On a lightly floured board roll each patty into a 6 x 8 inch oblong. Sprinkle half of each oblong with 2 tablespoons grated cheddar cheese and 1/4 teaspoon instant minced onion. Fold oblong and seal edges. Cut into 3/4-inch strips. Cut strips into 3-inch pieces. Cover 2 cookie sheets with heavy paper bags. Lay cheese strips on top of bags. Bake in 400°F oven 8 to 10 minutes. Watch carefully so straws don't over-brown.

POTATO-MUSHROOM CHOWDER

Mushrooms and potatoes are combined to make this yummy soup. Serve with a big green salad and you've got a super lunch or dinner.

1/2 lb. fresh mushrooms
2 tbs. butter
1 onion, chopped
1-1/2 cups diced potatoes
1 cup boiling water
2 cups milk
2 egg yolks, beaten

1/4 cup sherry or dry white wine
2 cups (1 pt.) sour cream
1/4 tsp. thyme leaves
dash cloves, mace
salt and white pepper
chopped parsley

Coarsely chop mushrooms. Melt butter in large saucepan. Saute mushrooms and onion 3 to 4 minutes. Add potatoes and water. Bring to boil. Cover and cook 10 minutes or until potatoes are tender. Add milk. Mix egg yolks with sherry and sour cream. Stir into soup. Heat but do not boil. Add cloves, mace, salt and pepper. Serve sprinkled with parsley. Makes 4 to 6 servings.

BOSTON CLAM CHOWDER

2 lbs. potatoes
4 tbs. (1/2 cube) butter
1 onion, chopped
1 stalk celery, chopped
1 tbs. salt
2 cans (10 ozs. ea.) whole baby clams, undrained
1 qt. whole milk
1 tsp. lemon juice
salt and lemon pepper
1/2 cup chopped parsley.

Peel and dice potatoes. Melt butter in large saucepan. Add onions, potatoes and celery. Saute until onions are transparent. Add enough water to cover potatoes. Cook, covered, until potatoes are tender, about 1/2 hour. Add salt, clams, milk and lemon juice. Simmer gently 1/2 hour. Add salt and lemon pepper. Serve sprinkled with chopped parsley. Complete the meal with French bread and dry white wine. Makes 4 servings.

VEGETABLE CLAM CHOWDER

3 tbs. butter
1 small onion, finely chopped
2 stalks celery, thinly sliced
1/2 green pepper, finely chopped
2 tbs. flour
2 pkg. (6 ozs. ea.) dry potato soup mix
2 cans (10 ozs. ea.) whole baby clams
1 pkg. (10 ozs.) frozen mixed vegetables

Melt butter in large saucepan. Add onion, celery and green pepper. Saute until tender. Sprinkle in flour. Cook 2 minutes. Prepare potato soup according to package directions. Combine with sauteed vegetables, clams and frozen vegetables. Gently simmer 10 minutes. Makes 6 servings.

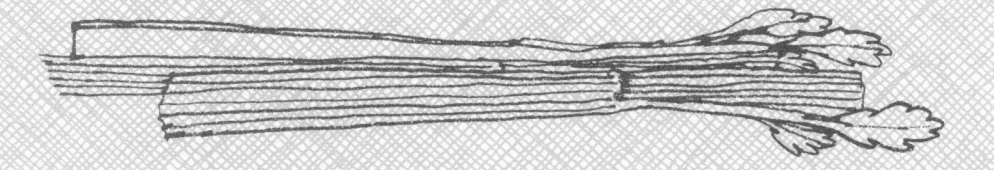

CINQUE TERRE CHOWDER

Cinque Terre, "five lands," is a charming, terraced region in Italy. Each terrace has a tiny village, about a mile apart, that can only be reached by a footpath along the cliffs above the beautiful, blue Mediterranean.

1/3 cup olive oil
2 cloves garlic, minced
1 can (8 ozs.) Italian tomatoes
1 tsp. oregano
1 bay leaf
salt and pepper

6 lobster tails, cut in bite-size pieces
1 cup dry white wine
12 large raw shrimp, deveined
12 fresh little neck clams, scrubbed
1/3 cup chopped parsley

Heat oil in large saucepan. Add garlic and saute 1 minute. Stir in tomatoes. Simmer 10 minutes. Add oregano, bay leaf, salt, pepper and lobster pieces. Bring to boil. Add wine, shrimp, clams and parsley. Cover. Reduce heat and simmer 7 to 10 minutes or until clams open. Makes 4 servings.

KAY'S SEAFOOD CHOWDER

Open-faced sandwiches complete this meal.

1 can (10-1/2 ozs.) New England-style clam chowder
1 can (10-1/2 ozs.) oyster stew
1 can (6-1/2 ozs.) minced clams
1 can (8 ozs.) oysters
1 can (6-1/2 ozs.) broken shrimp
1 soup can milk
1 soup can dry white wine
4 tbs. (1/2 cube) butter, sliced

Combine all ingredients except butter in large saucepan. Simmer 20 minutes. Serve with a pat of butter in each bowl. Makes 4 servings.

KATHY'S CATCHALL

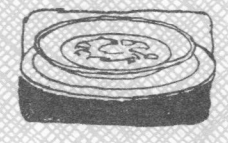

6 bacon slices, diced
1 onion, chopped
1-1/2 cups water
4 cups peeled diced potatoes
1 cup celery, diced
2 carrots, diced

1 chicken bouillon cube
1/2 tsp. thyme leaves
salt and pepper
1 lb. fresh or frozen fish fillets
3 cups milk
3 tbs. flour

Saute bacon and onions in large kettle. Drain off fat. Add water, potatoes, celery, carrots, bouillon, thyme, salt and pepper. Lay fish (if frozen, partially thaw first) on top. Bring to a boil. Cover and simmer 15 minutes, or until vegetables are tender and fish flakes when tested with a fork. Add 2-1/2 cups milk. Blend remaining milk with flour and stir into chowder. Bring to a boil. Turn off heat and let stand 1/2 hour to absorb flavors. Reheat gently to serving temperature. Makes 2-1/2 quarts.

DUMPLING, PASTA & BREAD SOUPS

WON TON SOUP

2 mushrooms, chopped
1/2 cup finely chopped cooked pork
1 tbs. finely chopped green onion
1 tsp. garlic salt
12 won ton skins
2 cans (10-3/4 ozs. ea.) condensed chicken broth
2 cans water
1/2 cup cooked pork, cut into thin strips
1/4 cup chopped fresh spinach

Mix mushrooms, chopped pork, green onion and garlic salt together well. Place a teaspoon of the mixture in the center of each won ton square. Moisten edges. Fold won ton in half. Press edges to seal. Moisten top right corner. Bring top left corner under right and press together. Pour broth and water into a large kettle and bring to boil. Carefully drop in won tons one at a time. Simmer 10 minutes. Serve with pork strips and spinach for garnish. Makes 4 to 6 servings.

40

GERMAN FARINA DUMPLING SOUP

3 tbs. butter
3 tbs. farina (cream of wheat)
dash nutmeg and white pepper
1 cup hot water
1 egg plus 1 egg yolk
3 tbs. chopped parsley
3 tbs. finely chopped spinach leaves
3 cans (14 oz. ea.) beef broth

Melt butter in small saucepan over medium-low heat. Add farina, nutmeg and pepper. Stir well until mixture starts bubbling. Add about 1/4 cup hot water. Stir until it gathers into a ball. Add a little more hot water, stirring constantly. Add 1/4 cup more water, stirring vigorously. Repeat process until mixture comes off sides of pan. Set aside to cool. When cool, beat in egg and egg yolk. Add chopped parsley and spinach. Pour beef broth into large saucepan. Bring to a boil, then reduce heat to simmer. Drop dumpling mixture by teaspoonfuls into gently simmering broth. Simmer 3 to 5 minutes. Makes 4 servings.

LIVER DUMPLING SOUP

Typical of Southern Germany, this delicious soup is well worth the effort.

3 large stale French rolls, sliced
1 tbs. butter
1/2 cup chopped onion
3 tbs. chopped parsley
1/4 lb. beef liver, cubed

1 thick (3/4 in.) slice slab bacon
salt and pepper
1 egg
1/4 cup flour
3 cans (14 ozs. ea.) beef broth

Cover bread with warm water and soak. Melt butter in small frying pan. Add onion and parsley. Saute until onions are transparent. Squeeze all the moisture out of bread, using a potato ricer if available, and set aside. Grind liver, bacon and onion mixture together in meat grinder. Stir in egg and mix well. Add flour, salt and pepper. Mix well. Pour beef broth into large saucepan. Bring to a boil, then reduce heat to simmer. Drop dumpling mixture by teaspoonfuls into gently simmering broth. Simmer 8 to 10 minutes. Makes 6 servings.

CHICKEN NOODLE SOUP

3 lb. chicken, cut up
2 qts. water
1 onion, chopped
2 carrots, sliced
2 celery stalks, sliced
1 tbs. salt
1/4 tsp. pepper
1 pkg. (10 ozs.) frozen vegetables, defrosted
1 pkg. (3 ozs.) Top Ramen noodles

Place chicken in kettle. Add water, onion, carrots, celery, salt and pepper. Bring to boil. Skim. Cover and simmer until tender, about 1-1/2 hours. Lift chicken from soup. When cool enough to handle, remove meat from bones and discard fat. Add meat to soup along with frozen vegetables and simmer until vegetables are cooked. Break noodles into fourths. Cook noodles according to package directions and drain well. Stir into soup and serve. Makes 6 servings.

SWISS BREAD AND CHEESE SOUP

This Swiss version of cheese soup is great after a long day of skiing.

1/2 lb. Gruyere cheese, grated
1 loaf (1 lb.) bread, toasted
4 cups boiling water
2 tbs. butter
salt and pepper
dash nutmeg
chopped chives

Layer bread and cheese in a large bowl. Pour boiling water over layers and let stand 10 minutes. Drain water from bowl. Press bread and cheese down firmly, squeezing out water. Drain again. Melt butter in frying pan. Add drained bread-cheese mixture to hot butter. Stir until fat comes out of cheese. Add salt, pepper and nutmeg. Sprinkle with chives and serve very hot. Makes 4 servings.

GARLIC SOUP

Marvelous when suffering with a cold or hangover.

3 tbs. oil
5 cloves garlic, sliced
6 slices French bread
3 cups water (approximately)
1 tbs. chopped parsley
4 eggs

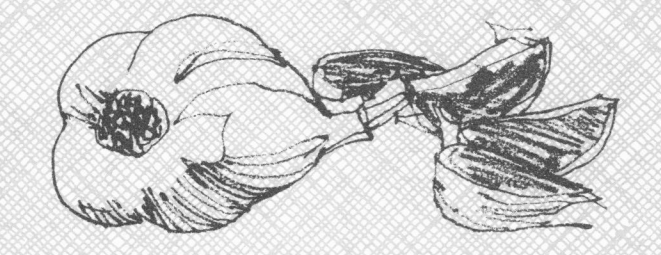

Heat oil in frying pan. Add garlic and saute until golden. Toast bread and cut into cubes. Add to pan with garlic and stir to coat with oil. Stir in water to cover bread. Add parsley. Simmer 15 minutes. Break eggs into garlic broth and poach until set, 3 to 5 minutes. Serve poached eggs in bowls. Ladle soup over eggs. Serve hot! Makes 2 to 4 servings.

HEARTY SOUPS

FRENCH ONION SOUP

3 tbs. butter
1 tbs. oil
5 cups thinly sliced onions
1 tsp. salt
1/4 tsp. sugar
3 tbs. flour
2 qts. boiling chicken stock
1/2 cup vermouth
1 cup Cognac
1 bay leaf
1/4 tsp. thyme
French Bread Slices, page 49

    Melt butter in heavy flame-proof casserole or Dutch oven. Add oil and onions. Cover and cook slowly 15 minutes. Uncover and raise heat to moderate. Stir in salt and sugar. Cook 30 minutes, stirring often until onions are dark brown and reduced to about 3/4 cup. Sprinkle in flour and cook 3 minutes. Stir in boiling stock, wine and

48

Cognac. Add seasonings. Simmer 30 minutes. At this point prepare French Bread Slices. Place bread on soup and bake, uncovered, in 375°F oven 10 minutes or until cheese melts. Serve at once. Makes 6 servings.

FRENCH BREAD SLICES

1 small narrow loaf French bread
butter
1/2 cup grated Parmesan, Swiss, Gruyere or Jack cheese

Slice bread into 1/2-inch thick slices. Butter slices and sprinkle with cheese. Place on top of soup. Bake, uncovered, in 375°F oven 10 minutes or until cheese melts.

AFTER-THE-FEAST TURKEY SOUP

1 turkey carcass
4 qts. water
4 chicken bouillon cubes
2 tbs. Spice Islands Beau Monde Seasoning
3 stalks celery, cut in chunks
3 carrots, cut in chunks
1/2 cup chopped parsley
1 onion, sliced
pepper
3 tbs. cornstarch
1 pkg. (10 ozs.) frozen peas and carrots, defrosted
6 egg yolks
1 cup (1/2 pt.) heavy cream
grated Parmesan cheese

Remove any meat remaining on the turkey carcass. Discard skin and fat. Cut meat into bite-size pieces. Set aside. Place carcass in large pot. Cover with water. Add

bouillon cubes, Beau Monde, celery, carrots, parsley, onion and pepper. Bring to a boil. Reduce heat. Cover and simmer 1 hour. Remove bones from broth. Cool and pick off any bits of meat. Strain broth. Press carrots and celery through a wire strainer. Measure broth and vegetables. There should be approximately 10 cups. Mix cornstarch with 3 tablespoons broth and add to soup. Bring to a boil, then reduce heat. Add peas and carrots. Beat egg yolks with cream. Gradually add 1 cup hot broth to egg mixture, stirring constantly. Slowly add all to simmering broth, stirring constantly. Add reserved turkey and cook over low heat until soup is slightly thickened. Add salt and pepper to taste. Pass Parmesan with soup. Makes 10 to 12 serving.

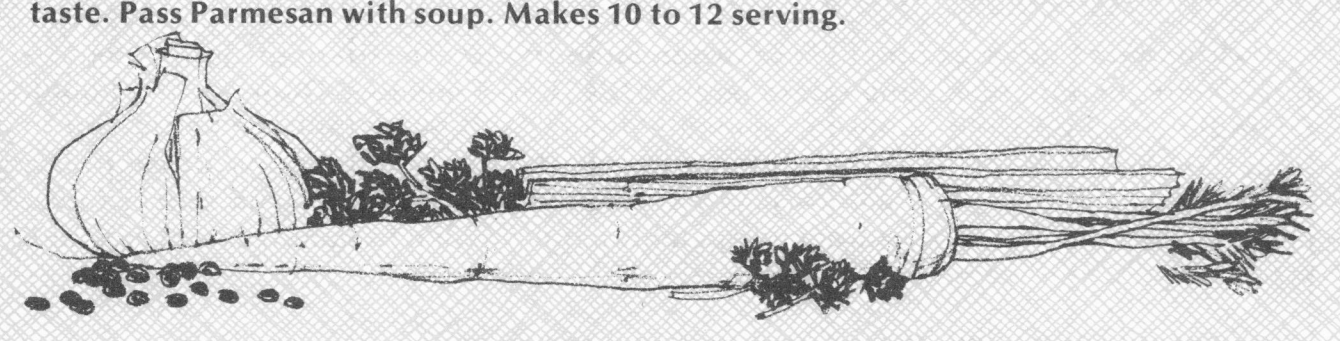

STEAK SOUP

2 lbs. round steak
2 cups carrots, sliced
2 cups celery, sliced
2 cups onions, chopped
8 cups water
1-1/2 tsp. salt
1/2 tsp. pepper
1 can (1 lb.) tomatoes

1/2 cup (1/4 lb.) butter
3/4 cup flour
1/4 cup Bovril
2 tbs. Worcestershire sauce
1 tsp. Accent
salt and pepper
1 pkg. (10 ozs.) frozen mixed vegetables

Grind meat twice as for chili. Brown in large frying pan. Drain off fat. Place carrots, celery, onions, water and salt in large kettle. Boil 5 minutes. Drain, saving liquid. Drain tomatoes and add liquid to vegetable liquid. Melt butter in large kettle. Stir in flour. Gradually add vegetable liquid, stirring constantly. Add Bovril, Worcestershire, Accent, salt and pepper. Combine meat, vegetables and tomatoes with sauce. Cover and simmer 20 minutes. Add frozen vegetables and simmer 10 minutes. Makes 6 to 8 servings.

GOULASH SOUP

1-1/2 lb. chuck roast
1/3 cup oil
1 onion, sliced
1 tbs. instant beef bouillon
1/2 cup water
1 tbs. wine vinegar
1 tsp. caraway seed
1/2 tsp. salt

1/4 tsp. pepper
1/4 tsp. marjoram
1 clove garlic, minced
1 can (16 ozs.) whole potatoes
1 can (16 ozs.) cut green beans, undrained
1 can (16 ozs.) sliced carrots, undrained
1 pkg. (10 ozs.) frozen peas

Trim meat and cut into 1-inch cubes. Heat oil in large kettle. Slowly brown meat. Add onion, beef bouillon, water, vinegar, caraway seed, salt, pepper, marjoram and garlic. Bring to boil. Cover and simmer 1 to 1-1/2 hours or until meat is tender. Drain potatoes and cut in half. Add to meat along with green beans, carrots and peas. Bring to boil. Reduce heat and simmer 20 minutes. Adjust seasonings and serve. Makes 6 servings.

PORTUGUESE SOUPAS

A contribution from my Portuguese Auntie Lou. This traditional soup is served for the Holy Ghost Festival. Fresh mint is a must. I grow it just for this soup.

4 lb. chuck roast
2 cloves garlic, slivered
4 quarts water
1 cup white wine
4 beef bouillon cubes
2 bay leaves

1 onion, minced
sprig fresh mint, minced
1 tsp. cumin
salt and pepper
thickly sliced French bread
fresh mint sprigs

Remove excess fat from meat. Poke garlic slivers into meat and place in Dutch oven. Add water, wine, bouillon, bay leaves, onion, mint, cumin, salt and pepper. Bring to a boil. Skim off foam. Simmer 3 to 4 hours or until meat comes off the bone. Remove bones and excess fat. Place a slice of French bread and sprig of mint in each bowl. Ladle broth and meat into bowls. Makes 6 to 8 servings.

BORSCH

One of the most familiar of the old-world soups. It makes an especially satisfying meal on a chilly evening.

2-1/2 lb. chuck roast
2 qts. water
2 bay leaves
6 peppercorns
salt and pepper
1 tsp. Accent
3 carrots, shredded
4 beets, peeled and shredded
2 potatoes, peeled and chopped
1-1/2 lbs. cabbage, shredded

2 tomatoes, peeled and chopped
1 green pepper, chopped
1 onion, chopped
1 tbs. oil
1 can (8 ozs.) tomato paste
juice of 1/2 lemon
1 tbs. sugar
2 cups (1 pt.) sour cream
fresh dill weed, minced
horseradish

Trim fat from roast. Place meat in large kettle. Add water, bay leaves, peppercorns, salt, pepper and Accent. Cover and simmer until tender, about 2 hours. Remove

meat from broth. Cover meat and keep warm. Add carrot, beets, potatoes, cabbage, tomatoes and green pepper to broth. Cook 45 minutes. Saute onion in oil. Add to broth along with tomato paste, lemon juice and sugar. Simmer 15 minutes. Adjust seasonings. Serve garnished with dollops of sour cream sprinkled with dill. Slice meat and serve separately with horseradish. Makes 8 to 10 servings.

MY MINESTRONE

After tasting many minestrones in Italy, I combined the best of each for my own version of a classic.

2 cups navy beans
2 lbs. beef shanks
12 cups water
2 tbs. salt
1 bay leaf
1 tsp. pepper
2 tsp. Italian seasoning
1 tsp. Accent
1 tsp. Spice Islands Beau Monde
1/2 cup red wine
1/2 cup olive oil

1 clove garlic, minced
2 carrots, sliced
4 stalks celery, chopped
2 cups tomato pulp or puree
2 cups cabbage, coarsely chopped
1 bunch chard, coarsely chopped
1 zucchini, sliced
2 cups cooked shell macaroni
1 tbs. wine vinegar
grated Parmesan cheese

Soak beans overnight or several hours. Place beef shanks in large kettle. Add water, salt, bay leaf and pepper. Bring to a boil and skim off foam. Cover and simmer 3

hours. Remove meat from kettle. When cool enough to handle trim away fat and bones. Return meat to kettle. Drain beans and add to meat. Cover and simmer 1 hour. Stir in Italian seasoning, Accent, Beau Monde and wine. Heat olive oil in skillet. Saute garlic, onions, carrot and celery until golden. Add to soup along with tomato pulp, cabbage and chard. Cover and cook over low heat 1 hour. Add zucchini an macaroni. Simmer 15 minutes. Blend in vinegar just before serving in large bowls with Parmesan cheese sprinkled over top. If soup becomes too thick, add a little water. Makes 6 to 8 servings.

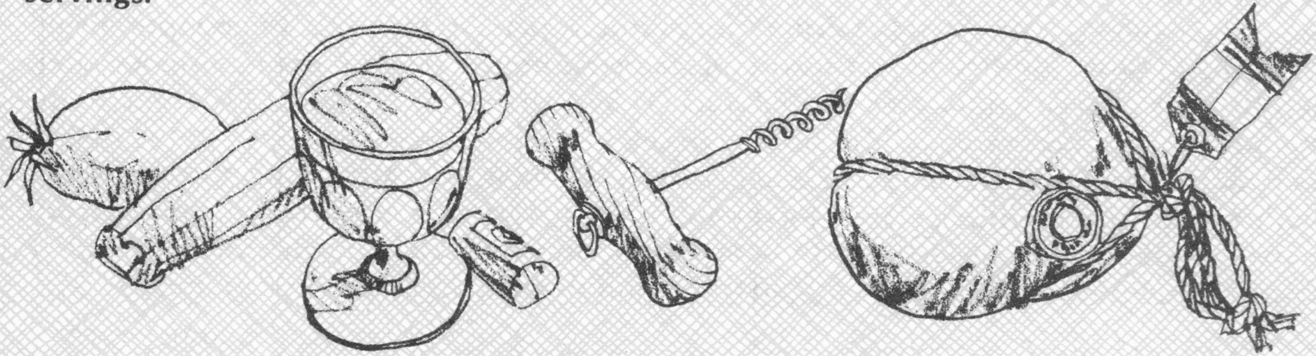

LENTIL BEEF SOUP

2 lbs. beef shanks
1 onion, chopped
5 qts. water
1 tsp. salt
1 tsp. pepper
1 pkg. (14 ozs.) lentils
3 carrots, sliced

3 stalks celery, chopped
1 clove garlic, minced
1/2 cup chopped parsley
1 tbs. salt
1 tbs. Worcestershire
grated Parmesan cheese
parsley sprigs

Place beef shanks in large kettle. Add onion, 2 quarts water, salt and pepper. Bring to boil and skim. Reduce heat. Cover and simmer 2 hours. While meat is cooking, soak lentils in 2 quarts cold water for 2 hours. When shanks are tender, lift from soup. Remove meat and marrow from bones. Break meat into serving pieces. Return meat and marrow to soup. Drain lentils and discard soaking water. Add lentils to soup along with 1 quart fresh, boiling water. Cover and simmer 1 hour. Add carrots, celery, garlic, parsley, salt and Worcestershire. Simmer 1 hour longer. Serve in bowls with a mound of grated Parmesan and a parsley sprig in the center of each. Makes 6 to 8 servings.

SOUP KETTLE SUPPER

A real family-pleaser and nice to have in the freezer for a busy day meal.

1-1/2 lbs. ground chuck
1 cup chopped onion
1 cup cubed raw potatoes
1 cup sliced carrots
1/2 cup diced celery
1 cup shredded cabbage
2-1/2 cups (No. 2 can) tomatoes
1/4 cup raw rice

1 small bay leaf
1/2 tsp. thyme
1/4 tsp. basil
2 tsp. salt
1/8 tsp. pepper
1-1/2 cups water
1-1/2 cups grated cheese

In kettle, cook beef with onion until lightly browned. Pour off fat. Add potatoes, carrots, celery, cabbage and tomatoes. Bring to boil. Pour in rice and stir. Add bay leaf, thyme, basil, salt, pepper and water. Cover and simmer 1 hour. Serve with grated cheese. Makes 6 servings.

SOPA DE ALBONDIGAS

Serve this Mexican favorite with Cheese Filled Tortillas, page 63.

1-1/2 lbs. chorizo (Mexican sausage)
1-1/2 lbs. ground round
2 cloves garlic, minced
1 tbs. parsley, minced
1 tsp. salt
1/2 cup soft bread crumbs
1 egg, beaten
1 tbs. chopped fresh mint

1/4 cup oil
1 onion, minced
3 qts. beef stock
3 carrots, sliced
3 zucchini, sliced
1 can (15 ozs.) Reese baby
   corn-on-the-cob, drained
fresh cilantro, coriander or Chinese parsley

Remove casing from chorizo. Mix sausage with ground round, 1 garlic clove, parsley, salt, bread crumbs, egg and mint. Shape into 1-inch balls. Heat 2 tablespoons oil in frying pan. Brown meatballs. Remove and drain on paper towels. Heat remaining oil in large kettle. Add onion and remaining garlic. Cook until onion is transparent. Add stock, carrots and zucchini. Bring to boil. Carefully drop meatballs into boiling

broth. Reduce heat, cover and simmer 30 minutes. Cool soup and skim excess fat from surface. Add baby corn and heat soup to serving temperature. Garnish with chopped cilantro. Makes 6 to 8 servings.

CHEESE FILLED TORTILLAS

1 dozen flour tortillas
2 cups grated cheddar
1/2 cube butter, softened

Place about 3 tablespoons grated cheese in center of each tortilla. Fold in half. Butter on both top and bottom sides. Heat frying pan and brown tortillas on both sides. Keep warm in low oven until serving time.

MEXICAN CHILI SOUP

Serve with hot buttered tortillas.

1 lb. ground beef
1 clove garlic, minced
1/2 green pepper, diced
1/2 onion, chopped
1 can (11 ozs.) chili beef soup
1 can (10-3/4 ozs.) tomato soup
2 soup cans water
salt and pepper
2 tbs. minced cilantro or Chinese parsley
1 cup (4 ozs.) grated cheddar cheese
 warm tortillas, buttered

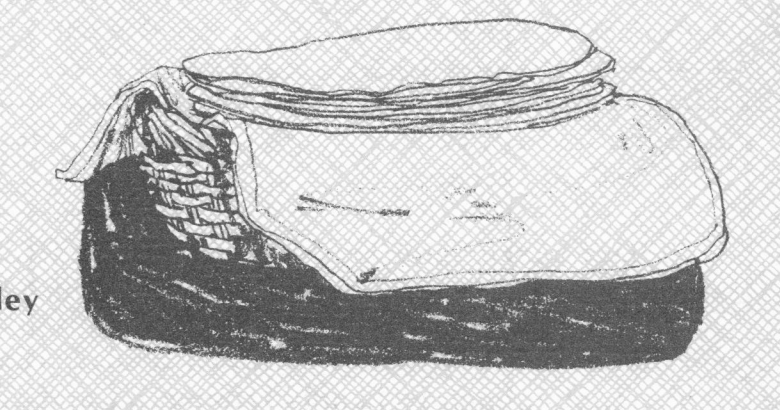

    Brown beef, garlic, green pepper and onion in skillet. Drain off fat. Stir in soups, water, salt, pepper and cilantro. Heat to serving temperature. Serve granished with grated cheese. Makes 4 to 6 servings.

FRANK'S GREEN BEAN SOUP

This delicious soup is an original from a man who loves to cook.

3 lbs. smoked ham
2 lbs. fresh green beans
1 large potato, diced
1 large onion, diced
2 large carrots, diced
1 tbs. summer savory

1 tbs. fresh dill
1 tbs. Accent
1 can (13 ozs.) evaporated milk
2 cups (1 pt.) sour cream
salt and pepper

Place ham in large kettle. Cover with water. Bring to boil and skim off foam. Cover and simmer 1 hour. Cut green beans into 1-inch pieces. Add to ham along with potato, onion, carrots, summer savory, dill weed and Accent. Cover and simmer 15 to 20 minutes or until vegetables are just tender. Turn off heat. Remove ham from kettle. When cool enough to handle remove fat and cut ham into bite-size pieces. Blend in milk and sour cream. Add salt and pepper. Heat gently to serving temperature. Makes 6 to 8 servings.

SAVORY BEAN SOUP

Serve with corn bread and a relish dish of olives, carrots, pickles and celery.

1 ham hock	2 cups solid-pack tomatoes
2 cups (1 lb.) pinto beans	1/2 cup chopped red pepper
6 cups water	1/2 cup chopped green pepper
2 tsp. seasoned salt	1 to 3 tsp. chili powder
1 onion, chopped	1 tbs. brown sugar
2 cloves garlic, mashed	1/2 tsp. dry mustard
1 bay leaf	salt and pepper
1/2 tsp. summer savory	2 tbs. chopped parsley

Place ham hock, beans, water and salt in large kettle. Cover and cook over low heat until beans are tender. Add onion, garlic, bay leaf, summer savory, tomatoes, peppers, chili powder, brown sugar, dry mustard, salt and pepper. Cover and simmer 1-1/2 hours. Serve garnished with parsley. Makes 4 to 6 servings.

SPLIT PEA SOUP WITH HAM

2 cups (1 lb.) green split peas
1-1/2 lbs. smoked ham hocks
3 qts. cold water
1 onion, chopped
2 stalks celery, chopped
2 carrots, chopped

3 sprigs parsley
1/4 tsp. marjoram
1 bay leaf
salt and pepper
dash cayenne pepper
2 drops green food coloring

Place split peas and ham hock in large kettle. Cover with cold water. Add onions, celery, carrots, parsley, marjoram and bay leaf. Bring to boil. Cover and simmer over low heat 2 to 3 hours or until peas are tender. Cool soup. Skim fat and remove ham hock. Remove meat from ham hock. Force soup through a coarse sieve, or pour into blender container. Cover and blend until smooth. Return soup to kettle. Add salt, pepper, cayenne, food coloring and ham. Bring to serving temperature over low heat. If a thicker soup is desired, mix 3 tablespoons butter with 3 tablespoons flour. Stir into soup and cook gently until mixture thickens. Serve with garlic bread. Makes 8 servings.

OLD-WORLD LENTIL SOUP

2 cups lentils
10 cups water
1 ham bone or shank
1 carrot, sliced
1 stalk celery, sliced
1 leek, sliced
2 green onions, minced
1 cup peeled diced potatoes
2 tbs. soy sauce
1/2 tsp. thyme

1 tbs. Worcestershire sauce
1 tsp. Spice Islands Beau Monde
1/2 tsp. savory
2 large frankfurters, sliced
1/4 cup (1/2 cube) butter
salt and pepper
1 tbs. wine vinegar
parsley
1 or 2 lemons, sliced

Soak lentils 3 hours. Do not drain. Bring to boil and add ham bone, carrot, celery, leek and green onions. Cover and simmer 3 hours. Add potatoes, thyme, soy sauce, Worcestershire, savory and Beau Monde. Cook 1 hour. Add frankfurters and heat. Stir in butter, salt, pepper, vinegar and parsley. Serve with a lemon slice floating in each bowl. Pass garlic French bread. Makes 8 to 10 servings.

69

HEARTY CABBAGE SOUP

1-1/2 cups chicken stock
5 wieners, thinly sliced
1/4 cup chopped onion
1/2 cup diced celery
1 potato, peeled and shredded
3 cups milk
2 cups finely chopped cabbage
2 tsp. salt
1 tsp. freshly ground pepper
1/2 tsp. caraway seed
1 tsp. brown sugar
1/2 cup half-and-half

Place stock, wieners, onion, celery and potato in large saucepan. Bring to a boil. Cover and simmer 15 minutes. Add milk, cabbage, salt, pepper, caraway seed and brown sugar. Simmer, but do not let boil, 25 minutes. Stir in half-and-half. Bring soup to serving temperature. Makes 4 servings.

SCOTCH BROTH

Serve with hot rolls and sweet butter.

1 cup barley	1 turnip, diced
11 cups water	2 carrots, chopped
3 lbs. lamb necks	4 celery stalks, chopped
1 tbs. salt	1 carrot, grated
3 tbs. butter	1/2 cup minced parsley
2 onions, chopped	salt and pepper

Soak barley overnight in 5 cups water. Cut meat from bones and trim away fat. Put meat and bones in a large kettle. Add 6 cups cold water and salt. Cover and simmer 1 hour. Add barley and soaking water. Cook until meat is tender, about 1-1/2 hours. Cool soup. Discard bones and cut meat into small pieces. Skim off fat. Melt butter in frying pan. Saute onions, turnip, chopped carrot and celery until golden. Add to soup. Simmer about 1 hour. Add grated carrot, parsley, salt and pepper to taste. Makes 8 servings.

DANISH KALE SOUP

A Danish friend shared this recipe. It's delicious.

2 lb. pork roast
2 carrots, peeled
2 potatoes, peeled
2 leeks

1/2 small celery root, peeled
1-1/2 cups chopped kale
3 tbs. flour
salt and pepper

Place pork, carrots, potatoes, leeks and celery root in large kettle. Add enough cold water to cover. Bring to a boil and cook until vegetables are tender. Remove vegetables from kettle and cut into cubes. Continue cooking pork until tender. When pork is done, remove from soup. Add kale and bring to a boil. Simmer until done. Mix flour with a little water. Blend into soup. Add cubed vegetables, salt and pepper. Slice pork. Serve soup in bowls. Pass hot, sliced pork, mustard and pumpernickel bread. Makes 4 servings.

PHILADELPHIA PEPPER POT

1/2 lb. honeycomb tripe
6 cups chicken stock
4 slices bacon
1 onion, chopped
1/2 cup chopped celery
1 green pepper, chopped
1 bay leaf

1 tsp. pepper
2 tbs. parsley, minced
2 tsp. salt
1 cup diced raw potatoes
2 tbs. soft butter
2 tbs. flour
1/2 cup heavy cream

Cook tripe for 1 hour in large saucepan with enough water to cover. Rinse and cut into 1/4 inch cubes. Place in large kettle. Add chicken stock and bring slowly to a boil. Cut bacon into small pieces. Fry until crisp. Saute onion, celery and green pepper in bacon drippings. Add to tripe. Stir in bay leaf, pepper, parsley, salt and potatoes. Cover and simmer 1 hour. Mix butter with flour and blend into soup mixture. Just before serving, stir in cream. Heat, but do not boil. Makes 6 to 8 servings.

QUICKIE SOUPS

QUICK CHICKEN STOCK

2 cans (13 ozs. ea.) Swanson Chicken Broth
1 carrot, sliced

1 stalk celery, sliced
parsley sprigs

Pour broth into saucepan. Bring to a boil. Add remaining ingredients. Cover. Simmer gently for 1/2 hour. Strain and use as desired. Makes about 1 quart.

GREEK LEMON SOUP

1/3 cup rice
6 cups chicken stock

2 egg yolks
juice of 1 large lemon

Wash rice in several waters and drain well. Bring chicken stock to a boil. Slowly add rice. Simmer 30 minutes. Beat egg yolks with lemon juice, thoroughly. Slowly beat 1 cup hot stock into egg-lemon mixture. Remove soup from heat. When boiling stops, add egg-broth mixture, stirring rapidly to prevent curdling. Continue stirring for a few seconds and serve immediately. Makes 4 servings.

EGG DROP SOUP

3 dried mushrooms
1 qt. chicken stock

1/2 cup cooked pork, shredded
2 eggs

1/2 tsp. Accent
1 whole green onion, minced

Soak mushrooms in warm water 20 minutes. Drain and chop. Bring broth to boil over medium heat. Add pork and mushrooms. Beat eggs well. Add to broth a spoonful at a time. Stir after each addition. Add Accent. Serve garnished with green onion. Makes 4 servings.

ORIENTAL GARDEN SOUP

2 cans (10-1/2 ozs. ea.) consomme
2 soup cans water
1/2 cup shredded lettuce

1/4 cup thinly sliced green onion
3 tbs. thinly sliced radishes
1 tsp. soy suace

Combine all ingredients in saucepan. Heat to serving temperature. Serve with rice crackers. Makes 4 to 6 servings.

QUICK 'N EASY ONION SOUP

7 onions, thinly sliced
3 tbs. butter
8 cans (10-1/2 ozs. ea.) beef broth

2 tbs. Worcestershire sauce
French Bread Slices, page 49

Brown onions in butter 20 minutes. Add broth and Worcestershire. Simmer 15 minutes. Ladle soup into oven-proof bowls. Place bread slices on top. Bake in 375°F oven until cheese melts. Makes 8 servings.

MOCK TURTLE SOUP

1 can (10-1/2 ozs.) condensed mock turtle soup
1 can (10-1/2 ozs.) condensed pea soup
1 can (10-1/2 ozs.) consomme

2 soup cans water
1/4 cup dry sherry

Combine soups in large saucepan. Gradually stir in water. Bring to boil. Reduce heat and add sherry just before serving. Makes 6 servings.

SENEGALESE SOUP

2 cans (10-1/2 ozs. ea.) cream of chicken soup
1/8 tsp. each ground coriander and cumin

1/2 tsp. curry powder
2 soup cans milk

In saucepan thoroughly blend soup, coriander, cumin and curry. Gradually stir in milk. Heat slowly. Serve hot, or chill mixture at least 4 hours before serving. Makes 4 to 6 servings.

VIRGINIA PEANUT SOUP

2 cans (10-1/2 ozs. ea.) cream of chicken soup
2 soup cans milk
1 cup crunch-style peanut butter

Empty soup into saucepan. Slowly blend in milk a little at a time. Add peanut butter. Stir over low heat until warm and well blended. Makes 4 to 6 servings.

79

TOMATO BOUILLON

A lovely blending of flavors to sharpen appetites before a hearty meal.

3 cups tomato juice
1 thick onion slice
1 stalk celery, sliced
1 bay leaf
2 whole cloves
1 can (10-1/2 ozs.) consomme
salt and pepper
thin lemon slices

Combine tomato juice, onion, celery, bay leaf and cloves in large saucepan. Bring to boil. Cover and simmer 25 minutes. Strain. Add consomme, salt and pepper. Heat to serving temperature. Ladle into soup bowls and float a lemon slice on each serving. Makes 4 to 6 servings.

CHEESE AND ONION SOUP

Serve with thick slices of your favorite crusty bread.

1 qt. milk
1/4 cup butter
4 onions, finely chopped
1/4 cup flour
1 cup (4 ozs.) grated Gruyere, Emmentaler or cheddar cheese
salt and pepper

Scald milk. Melt butter and brown onions. Blend in flour. Cook, stirring, 1 minute. Remove from heat. Gradually add milk. Return to heat and boil 1 minute, stirring constantly. Add cheese, salt and pepper. Stir until cheese melts. Makes 4 servings.

CHEDDER CHEESE SOUP

1/4 cup butter
1/2 cup minced onion
1/2 cup flour
1 qt. milk
1 qt. chicken stock
1/2 cup minced carrot
1/2 cup minced celery
dash paprika
1 cup diced sharp cheddar cheese
salt and white pepper

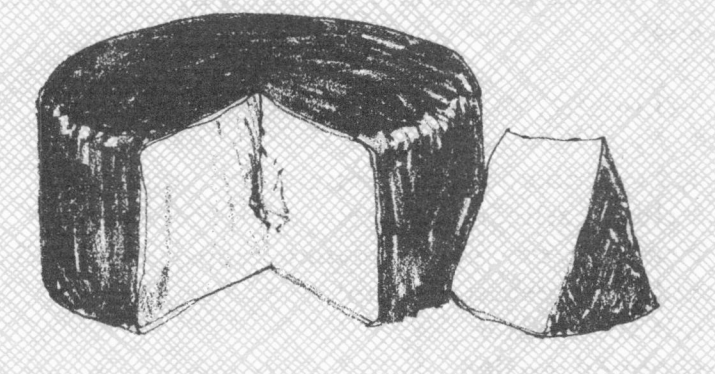

Melt butter in large saucepan. Add onion and cook until transparent, but not browned. Blend in flour. Gradually stir in milk, broth, carrot, celery, and paprika. Simmer, stirring, until mixture thickens and bubbles. Reduce heat. Add cheese and stir until melted. Add salt and pepper. Simmer gently 15 minutes, stirring occasionally. Serve with assorted crackers and apple slices. Makes 6 to 8 servings.

GARBANZO SOUP

I was introduced to this soup while visiting a Basque friend in San Sabastian, Spain.

3 chorizos (Mexican sausages), sliced
1/2 cup diced onion
1/2 cup diced green pepper
1 clove garlic, minced
2 cans (16 ozs. ea.) garbanzo beans, undrained
1/2 tsp. crushed oregano
salt and pepper
chopped parsley

Brown chorizos, onion, green pepper and garlic together. Add garbanzos and juice, oregano, salt and pepper. Simmer 15 minutes. Garnish with parsley. Makes 4 servings.

NEPTUNE'S CHOWDER

1 can (15 ozs.) Snow's Clam Chowder
1 can (10-1/2 ozs.) cream of mushroom soup
1 can (13 ozs.) evaporated milk, undiluted
1 can (4 ozs.) mushrooms
1 can (6-1/2 ozs.) minced clams
2 cans (5-1/2 ozs. ea.) crabmeat
6 ozs. fresh cooked shrimp
1 cup chopped parsley
1/4 cup dry sherry
1 tsp. Worcestershire sauce
dash Tabasco
1/4 cup butter

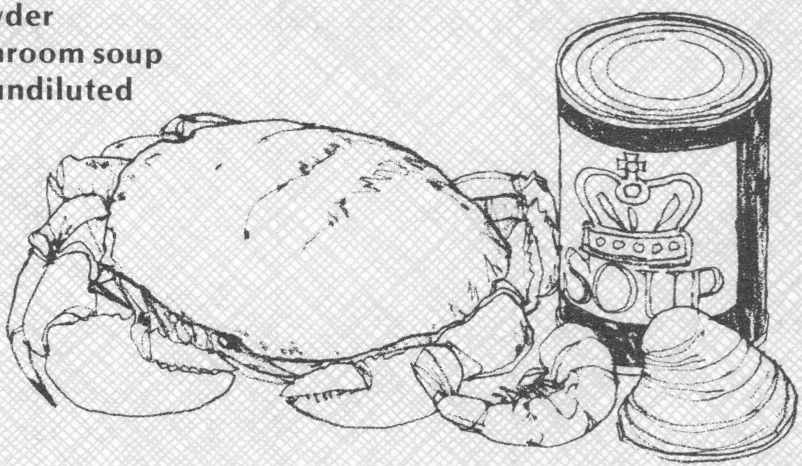

Combine clam chowder, mushroom soup, evaporated milk, mushrooms and clams in a large saucepan. Heat slowly, but do not let boil, about 15 minutes. Add crabmeat, shrimp, parsley, sherry, Worcestershire, Tabasco and butter. Heat to serving temperature. Makes 4 servings.

HOT BOYSENBERRY SOUP

Scandinavians serve fruit soup hot for breakfast and lunch, or chilled for the evening meal dessert.

1 cup water
2/3 cup sugar
4 cups fresh boysenberries
1-1/2 tbs. cornstarch
2 tbs. water
1 cup heavy cream

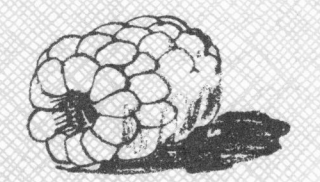

Mix water and sugar. Bring to a boil. Add berries. Bring to boil again. Simmer 2 minutes. Mix cornstarch and water. Add to soup. Serve hot with cream poured on top. Makes 4 servings.

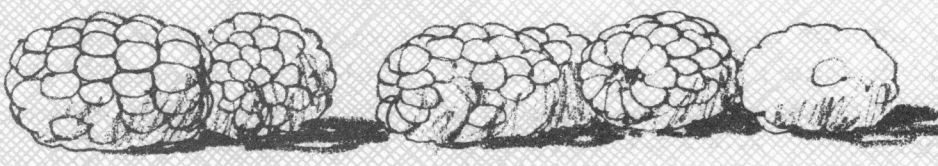

INDEX